Database Management System

Database Management System

An Evolutionary Approach

Jagdish Chandra Patni

Hitesh Kumar Sharma

Ravi Tomar

Avita Katal

CRC Press

Taylor & Francis Group

Boca Raton London New York

CRC Press is an imprint of the
Taylor & Francis Group, an **informa** business

A CHAPMAN & HALL BOOK

First edition published 2022
by CRC Press
6000 Broken Sound Parkway NW, Suite 300, Boca Raton, FL 33487-2742

and by CRC Press
2 Park Square, Milton Park, Abingdon, Oxon, OX14 4RN

CRC Press is an imprint of Taylor & Francis Group, LLC

© 2022 Jagdish Chandra Patni, Hitesh Kumar Sharma, Ravi Tomar, Avita Katal

Library of Congress Cataloging-in-Publication Data
Names: Patni, Jagdish Chandra, author. | Sharma, Hitesh Kumar, author. |
Tomar, Ravi, author. | Katal, Avita, author.
Title: Database management system : an evolutionary approach / Jagdish Chandra Patni,
Hitesh Kumar Sharma, Ravi Tomar, Avita Katal.
Description: First edition. | Boca Raton : Chapman & Hall/CRC Press, 2022. |
Includes bibliographical references and index. |
Summary: "This book explains the basic and advance concepts necessary for designing and implementing database systems and database applications. It puts emphasis on the core technical part of database modelling and design. It is meant to be used as a textbook for a technical course in database systems at the undergraduate and graduate level"– Provided by publisher.
Identifiers: LCCN 2021037797 (print) | LCCN 2021037798 (ebook) | ISBN 9780367244934 (hardback) | ISBN 9781032183466 (paperback) | ISBN 9780429282843 (ebook)
Subjects: LCSH: Database management. | Database design.
Classification: LCC QA76.9.D3 P34875 2022 (print) |
LCC QA76.9.D3 (ebook) | DDC 005.75/65–dc23
LC record available at https://lccn.loc.gov/2021037797
LC ebook record available at https://lccn.loc.gov/2021037798

ISBN: 978-0-367-24493-4 (hbk)
ISBN: 978-1-032-18346-6 (pbk)
ISBN: 978-0-429-28284-3 (ebk)

DOI: 10.1201/9780429282843

Typeset in Minion
by codeMantra

Instructor support material available on the website: https://www.routledge.com/9780367244934

Contents

Preface

DATA HAVE BEEN AN INTEGRAL PART OF ANY information system; the foundation of an information system itself comes from data. Handling data is a critical task when it comes to a scale, and the traditional way of handling this data using files is already a decade-old story. Specialized sets of software have emerged as a boon to data handling, and these specialized sets of software are what we call database management systems (DBMSs). The popularity, ease of use, and rapid adoption of DBMSs made it imperative for us to discuss them for novice as well as experienced users.

This book *Database Management System – An Evolutionary Approach* presents ideas, plans, applications, and advancements of DBMSs in an extremely extensive way. The sections are written in an exceptionally basic language with examples. In this book, an excessive number of figures are utilized for clarification with the goal that readers can undoubtedly comprehend the ideas presented. This book guarantees to fill the gap between hypothetical learning and down-to-earth execution of ideas of information bases. We trust that this book will be helpful to all manner of readers. We invite readers to send in their ideas for improving the book.

Chapter summaries:

Chapter 1: This chapter gives the basics of databases and details the roles of users and administrators.

Chapter 2: This chapter describes various data models and their applications in industry and academia with the help of examples.

Chapter 3: This chapter presents relational DBMS with its terminologies and various types of keys used. It then goes on to explain relational algebra and Codd's rules.

Chapter 4: This chapter explains the concepts of the most popular conceptual models, namely, ER diagram and EER diagram, with their reduction into tables.

Chapter 5: In this chapter, the concepts of normalization are discussed with the detailed explanation of normal forms, i.e., first, second and third and BCNF.

Chapter 6: Here, the concepts of SQL are discussed with its types: data definition language, data manipulation language, data control language, and data retrieval language.

Chapter 7: This chapter delves into the advanced concept of SQL and PL/SQL explaining the concepts of if-else, loop, procedure, functions, cursors, triggers, etc.

Chapter 8: This chapter explores the transaction processing system and concurrency control with its various types. It discusses the concurrent schedule and the concept of serializability. It explains the various protocols used in the concurrency control and database backup and recovery protocols.

Extended case studies are provided that aim to assist the reader in exploring more dimensions of DBMSs as a solution to larger domains.

We hope that this book offers you an amazing experience at hands-on learning that you can refer back to anytime you need a refresher.

Authors

Jagdish Chandra Patni is an associate professor at the School of Computer Science, University of Petroleum and Energy Studies, Dehradun, Uttarakhand, India. He earned his PhD in the area of high-performance computing in 2016. He competed his M.Tech. and B.Tech. in 2009 and 2004, respectively. Dr. Patni is actively working in the research areas of database systems, high-performance computing, software engineering, machine learning, and IoT. He has authored more than 50 research articles in journals and conferences of national and international repute. Dr. Patni has authored more than five books and book chapters with international publishers such as Springer. He is an active guest editor/reviewer of various refereed international journals. He has delivered 15 keynote/guest speeches in India and abroad. He has organized multiple conferences/seminars/workshops/FDPs in India and abroad. Dr. Patni has been awarded Researcher of the Year 2021 by the Government of Uttarakhand, Teacher of the Year 2020 by the Government of Uttarakhand, Best Paper Award by Hosei University, Tokyo, Japan in 2020, and many more. He is a senior member of IEEE, Member of ACM, MIE, IEANG, IACSIT, and Vigyan Bharti, among others.

Hitesh Kumar Sharma is an associate professor at the School of Computer Science, University of Petroleum and Energy Studies, Dehradun, Uttarakhand, India. He earned his PhD in database performance tuning in 2016. He has completed his M.Tech. in 2009. His research interests are in machine learning, deep learning, image processing, and IoT with blockchain. He has authored more than 60 research articles in journals and conferences of national and international repute. Dr. Sharma has authored three books and book chapters with international publishers such as Springer. He is an active guest editor/reviewer of various refereed international journals. He has delivered various keynote/ guest speeches in India and abroad. He has many certifications in DevOps in the last 2 years. He has also been granted three patents in his academic career in the past few years.

Ravi Tomar is an assistant professor in the School of Computer Science at the University of Petroleum and Energy Studies, Dehradun, India. He is an experienced academician with a demonstrated history of working in the higher education industry. He is skilled in programming, computer networking, stream processing, Python, Oracle database, C++, core Java, J2EE, RPA, and CorDApp. His research interests include wireless sensor networks, image processing, data mining and warehousing, computer networks, big data technologies, and VANET. Dr. Tomar has authored more than 51 papers in different research areas, filed two Indian patents, edited two books, and authored four books. He has conducted training sessions for corporations nationally and internationally on Confluent Apache Kafka, Stream Processing, RPA, CordaApp, J2EE, and IoT to clients including KeyBank, Accenture, Union Bank of Philippines, Ernst and Young, and Deloitte. Dr. Tomar is officially recognized as an instructor for Confluent and CordApp. He has organized various international conferences in India, France, and Nepal. He has been awarded a Young Researcher in Computer Science and Engineering by RedInno, India in 2018.

 **Avita Katal** is an assistant professor (SS) in the Department of Virtualization, School of Computer Science, University of Petroleum and Energy Studies, Dehradun, Uttarakhand, India. She earned her B.E. degree from the University of Jammu in Computer Science Engineering in 2010 and M.Tech. degree in 2013. She is currently pursuing her PhD in the area of cloud computing from the University of Petroleum and Energy Studies, Dehradun, India. Ms. Katal's research interests are in the areas of cloud computing, mobile ad hoc networks, blockchain, IoT, and artificial intelligence, among others. She has published various research papers in renowned conferences and journals, and has also served as a reviewer for various conferences and journals. She has a keen interest in improving the teaching pedagogies and has participated in various faculty development programs. She is also currently pursuing a Postgraduate Certificate in Academic Practice (PGCAP) from the University of Petroleum and Energy Studies, Dehradun, India.

CHAPTER 1

Database Basics

1.1 INTRODUCTION AND HISTORY OF DATABASES

Data is defined as raw bits or pieces of information that lack context. It doesn't lead to any learning until processed. Data can be quantitative or qualitative in nature. Quantitative data is generally numerical, whereas qualitative data is descriptive in nature.

Quantitative data is the result of a measurement, count, or some other mathematical calculation. Data when brought to the context gives information, which can be further aggregated and analyzed to help us make decisions, and thus gain knowledge. For example, quantitative data such as 20, 30, 40, and 60 does not mean anything to us until we add context to it saying that this data is the number of students for specific classes. Thus, now it becomes information that can be used to set certain rules, policies, etc. in a university.

The main goal of the information system is to convert data into information in order to generate knowledge and thus further help in decision-making. Databases are designed for such purposes.

A database is defined as an organized collection of related information. All data stored in a database is related. For example, a student database should not hold information about airline reservation systems. The general-purpose software package that manages the data stored in a database is called a database management system (DBMS).

In the early years of computer generation, punch cards were used for data input and output and even for data storage. Databases came along much later. The first computer programs were developed in the 1950s [1]. At that time, computers were nothing but giant machines or, we can say, calculators that computed the results. The data was considered to be non-important or just as a leftover of the processing information, but as computers started being available commercially, this data, which was considered to be non-important, is now being used by business people for real-world purposes.

The integrated database system, the first DBMS, was designed in the 1960s by Charles W. Bachman [2]. IBM also at that time created a database system called IMS. Both these databases were considered as the predecessor of navigational databases (records/objects are found by following references from other objects). These databases became possible because of the advent of disks in contrast to magnetic tape and punched cards which were being used previously. The data access in such systems was possible only sequentially.

With time, the speed and flexibility of computers increased, and this led to the advent of many general-purpose database systems. This required a standardization, which led to the formation of the Database Task Group by Bachman who took responsibility for the standardization and design of a database. The group presented the "CODASYL approach" standard in 1971 [3]. The approach was complicated and required manual intervention as well as training. The records here could be accessed/searched through

- Primary key (CALC key),

- Moving relationships from one record to another (sets), and

- Scanning the records in sequential order.

This approach became less popular over time because of its complex nature. Many easier systems came onto the market.

Edgar Codd, an employee of IBM, came up with a new idea for storing data and processing of large databases with his paper titled "A Relational Model of Data for Large Shared Data Banks" [4]. Unhappy with the searching mechanism of CODASYL and IMS of IBM, he used a table with fixed length records unlike in CODASYL where records were stored in a linked-list form. Michael Stonebraker and Eugene Wong from UC Berkeley showed interest and researched relational database systems under a project called INGRES in 1974 [5]. The project demonstrated that the model is practical as well as efficient. They worked with QUEL query language, and it led to the creation of systems such as Ingres Corp., MS SQL Server, Sybase, Wang's PACE, and Britton-Lee. Another relational database system prototype was created by IBM called System R, which used SEQUEL query language and contributed to the development of SQL/DS, DB2, Allbase, Oracle, and NonStop SQL. IBM came up with SQL in 1974 (SQL became ANSI and OSI standards in 1986 and 1987), which replaced QUEL and many more functional query languages.

P. Chen introduced a new database model in 1976, which focused on data application rather than on logical table structure and was called entity-relationship model [6].

The success of relational database models boosted the database market, while the popularity of network and hierarchical database models slumped. IBM DB2 was the flagship product, and other products such as PARADOX, RBASE 5000, RIM, Dbase III and IV, OS/2 Database Manager, and Watcom SQL were also developed. Application development client tools were also released in the early 1990s along with the creation of object database management systems. Tools released include Oracle Developer, PowerBuilder, and VB. In the late 1990s, increase in the use of Internet database resulted in the release of many Internet database connectors such as Front Page, Active Server Pages, Java Servlets, Dream Weaver, ColdFusion, Enterprise Java Beans, and Oracle Developer 2000. Some open-source solutions provided for the Internet included CGI, GCC, MySQL, and Apache.

Relational database management systems (RDBMSs) though were efficient to store as well as process structured data. But with the passage of time and increased use of Internet for social media, unstructured data (such as photos, music, and videos) became more common. A RDBMS was not designed to handle such schema-less and nonrelational data. In addition, Structured Query Language also known as NoSQL came into the picture for catering to the needs of fast processing of unstructured data. It is a nonrelational data model and uses a distributed database system. It can handle structured as well as unstructured data. Although they have become very popular nowadays because of their high flexibility, scalability, lower costs, and capability to handle all kinds of data, they have some disadvantages associated too, one being that they are highly resource-intensive, that is, they require a high amount of RAM and CPU, and they lack tech support too (Figure 1.1).

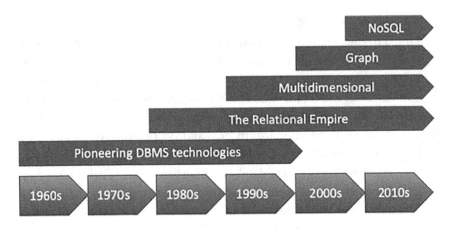

FIGURE 1.1   Evolution of database systems.

1.2 DATA AND INFORMATION

1.2.1 Data

In Section 1.1, we discussed data in general; data in the context of database is defined as an individual entity or a set of entities stored. The data stored in a database is generally organized in the form of rows and columns. Let's take an example of a bank database, which has customer details, including their name, address, and telephone number. These attributes or columns of the bank database are simply data as they are not contributing to something that can help us make any or obtain any kind of important information.

The database data has the following features/characteristics associated with it:

Shared: Since the data in a database will be used to derive some information for the users, it should be shareable among users as well as applications.

Persistence: The data in the database resides permanently meaning that even if the process that generated the data or used it ends, the data still exists in the storage beyond the scope of the process creating or using it.

Integrity: Data stored in a database should be correct with respect to the real world.

Security: Data stored in a database should not be accessed by unauthorized users.

Consistency: The values stored in a database corresponding to the real world should also be consistent to the relation of those values.

Nonredundancy: No two data items should represent the same world entity.

Independence: The data representation at internal, conceptual, or external level should be independent of each other. Change in one level should not affect the other.

1.2.2 Information

In today's age of information explosion, where we are being bombarded with too much data, information forms a very important resource, which provides a competitive edge to the organizations and businesses who are capable of processing it and using it to make decisions for surviving and excelling in the competitive market. As said by William Pollard, "Information is a source of learning. But unless it is organized, processed, and available to the right people in a format for decision-making, it is a burden, not a benefit" [7]. Refined data is information. The existing high-end systems have made it possible to manipulate and modify data. Information systems using such machines can thus work in different domains, for example, they can be used for building recommendation systems, engineering calculations, medical diagnosis, etc.

Information consists of data, images, text, documents, and voice. Data is processed through models to get information. The information generated reaches the recipient well in time and is used further for making decisions. These decisions can trigger other events and actions that generate large amounts of scattered data, which is captured again and sent as an input, and thus the cycle continues (Figure 1.2).

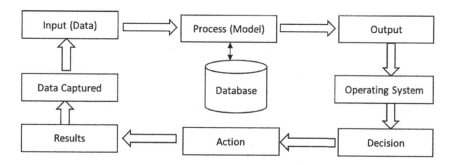

FIGURE 1.2   Information cycle.

People are overloaded with misinformation. Thus, quality information is required. Quality information means accurate, timely, and relevant information.

Accuracy: Accuracy of information refers to the veracity of it. It means there should be no manipulated or distorted information. It should clearly convey the meaning of the data it is based on.

Timeliness: The information must reach the recipient within the needed time frame. The information may be of no use if it arrives late.

Relevancy: Relevancy of the information means that the information which may be relevant for one user may not be relevant for another even though it might have been accurate as well as timely. For example: A person who wants to know the configuration of the computer model may get the answer as "The price for the model is Rs 40,000". Though the information is correct and timely, it is of no use.

1.3 DATABASE

Database, in general, is defined as a collection of related data. This stored data has some relation or mapping to real-world scenarios, or we can say that it has some universe of discourse (miniworld). In addition, the stored data is coherent and not randomly arranged in nature, holding some implicit information. The stored data has some values, which are entered or fetched from it intended for use by a set of users or applications.

The basic purpose of having a database is to operate on a large amount of stored data in order to provide information out from it. Dynamic websites on the World Wide Web make use of databases. Booking hotel rooms from some trip planning websites is one such example.

A database can be of any size or complexity. If we consider the database of students in a department, it may consist of a few hundred records of different attributes/columns such as name, address, and roll no. But when we consider the university to be the miniworld of this database, this data may have thousands of entries, and then if the miniworld changes to universities in a country, the number of entries may be in lakhs.

The IRCTC system for booking rail tickets is one such example of database where millions of users try to book, cancel, or check the status of the tickets and trains. This system is used to book on average 5 lakh tickets per day; around 1.2 lakh people can use this IRCTC site at one time, and in a year, 31 crore tickets are booked [8]. IRCTC has generated higher revenue than commerce giants Flipkart and Amazon India. Thus, the database size and complexity very much depend on the miniworld it is being used in.

1.4 NEED FOR A DATABASE

A database can be defined as a collection of data, which is designed to be used by different people. The question which will come to our mind again and again is why we need a database when we already have the data for an organization stored in disks and tapes in the form of files. The question itself has the answer. The data stored in disks and tapes is always dispersed and hence difficult to control. Some other important reasons that move us toward adoption of databases for organization are as follows:

- Duplication of data and effort from the users' end.

- Redundancy of data.

- Data is hardcoded in applications.

- Inconsistent data.

- Data integrity issues.

- Data security issues.

- Concurrency issues.

- Nonuniform backup and recovery methods.

- Interdependence between data and programs.

- Ad hoc data management techniques.

- Ad hoc representation of relationships.

1.5 FILE-BASED DATA MANAGEMENT SYSTEM

A file management system also known as a file system is a traditional or, we can say, an ancient way in which data files were stored on hard drives. A file is basically a collection of bytes stored together as an individual entity. Initially, when there were no computers the data was stored or maintained on registers, and any modification, access, or updating of records stored was difficult. With the advent of computers, all the work was shifted to computer drives where the data was stored. It was stored in the form of isolated files at different locations in the drive. In order to access these files, the user had to manually follow a path to reach the destination file.

Although the method used was better in comparison to the manual record maintenance, it also suffered from many problems as follows:

- **Data Redundancy** is sporadic, and cannot be controlled, leading to wastage of space and duplication of efforts at the user end. Since the data is being created by different programmers/users from various departments over a longer period of time, it is quite possible that the data may be repeated across these files.

- **Data Inconsistency** arises because of data redundancy. Let's say, a student's address is maintained in two different files. When the student's address changes, it needs to be updated in both the files. But if only the record in one of the files is updated, it leads to confusion of which of the data is correct as both the files will be having two different addresses for the same student.

- **Data Isolation** is another big challenge faced by the file-based data management system. Let's say, we have to get all the details of a student such as his fee clearance, hostel accommodation information, grade sheet, and library book details. In a file-based system, each of the departments involved here, that is, finance department, hostel department, examination department, and library department, will have its own files with different formats stored at different locations on the drive. Only when the details of these files are gathered, a program can be written to get the single student report required. This requires a lot of effort from the programmer as the data is isolated from one another, and there is no link between it.

- **Data Integrity** is another big problem. It refers to the correctness of the data being inserted in the file. Unlike in DBMS, there is no such direct facility to check the constraints in the data being entered. It is possible in a file-based data management system with the help of application programs only.

- **Data Security** is a challenge because a file-based data management system cannot provide privileges at the record level. Although files can be password-protected, once the file accepts the password, the entire content of the file is available. There is no discrete control.

- **Atomicity** means that the transaction should occur completely, or if it fails due to some reasons, the system should be able to roll back to the last consistent state. However, this is difficult to be achieved by a file-based data management system.

- **Dependency** of application programs on the file data is another issue. This means that if the content of the file is changed, it affects the application programs that were designed to access the content from the file too.

1.6 DATABASE SYSTEM

A database can be created manually if it is small in size. Generally, depending on the size of the database, a group of application programs are needed for its creation and maintenance. Such a database is called a DBMS. This set of programs help in defining, creating, manipulating, and sharing the database between multiple users and applications. Defining the database generally includes specifying the data types, constraints, and structures of the data we are storing in the database. This data is generally called metadata or catalog or dictionary. Storing the data on storage media that can be managed by a DBMS is construction. Fetching and updating the data in a database using some query language is manipulation of the data. Sharing includes access of the data in the database simultaneously or parallelly by multiple users and application programs. Database management software has to provide another important functionality, i.e., protection. Protection includes protecting the data against hardware and software malfunctions along with protection against unauthorized users and applications. A database and database management software together are called a database system.

1.6.1 Database System Components

As discussed in the above section, a database system comprises database and management software. So, the components of the database system can be categorized as follows [9]: hardware, software, data, procedures, database access language (query language in general), users, and database.

Hardware basically refers to computer, which includes hard disks for storing the data, magnetic tape, etc. for backing up the stored data, I/O channels for transferring the data to memory which can be RAM or ROM, keyboard for input and monitor for output, etc. Database **software** basically refers to the set or collection of programs which is used to access, manipulate, or update the data stored on the storage media in a database. The software is capable of understanding the database access language and interprets it into actual database commands to be executed on the database stored on hardware.

Data is the main resource around which all the database management software are designed. Data about data called **metadata** is part of a DBMS. This metadata generally contains information such as data types, size, constraints on the data, and relation with other data items stored in the database.

Procedures include steps followed to setup and install a DBMS, login and logout facility in a DBMS, management of a database, taking backups of data stores, and generating reports.

Database access language is the most important component of a database because there is no use of data stored if there is no way of gathering information from it. Database access language is used to access, delete, insert, and update data in a database. Users write commands in these languages, which are further submitted to a DBMS for translation and execution on hardware.

If we talk of databases that are small in size and are used for personal work, they have very few people associated, i.e., the same person designs, maintains, and uses the database. But the databases that are used at a larger level, for example at the organization level, there are many people involved such as those who work on the scene, i.e., who use the database to access information and those who work behind the scene, the ones who are involved in the maintenance of this data.

Database administrators (DBAs) are generally responsible for managing the resources. In a database system, the main resource is the database itself, DBMS being the secondary resource. The DBA here is responsible for ensuring the authorized access to the database, coordinating the use of the database, and monitoring the usage of the database. He is also responsible for purchasing the required hardware and software necessary for proper functioning of the database, which further includes database response time. The administrator is also responsible for security breaches and threats to the database.

Database designers are responsible for interacting with the users and understanding their requirements before actually storing the data in a database. They build views that meet database and processing requirements, then these views designed after interacting with potential user groups are integrated to form a single design. Generally, database designers are on the same staff as that of DBAs. Once the design is completed, these people share the responsibilities of DBAs.

The **users** require access to the database for querying, updating, and generating reports. But they can be further categorized on the basis of their frequency of access to the database.

The end users access the database less frequently, or each time they access the data for different information. They make use of sophisticated database query language to get this information, for example, managers who access the database occasionally. Such users are categorized as **casual end users.** These users learn few facilities, which they use repeatedly.

The second category known as **parametric or naive users** involves the ones who constantly access, manipulate, and update the database using canned transactions. Canned transactions are well programmed and tested. Bank tellers who constantly update the accounts after debit and credit and on opening of various types of accounts fall under this category. Naïve users need to understand few or very little facilities of the DBMS but have to understand the use of interfaces to execute canned transactions.

The third category consists of users such as scientists, engineers, and business analysts who form the **sophisticated users** category. They make themselves very well aware of the DBMS and then use it to meet their complex requirements. These users learn about the maximum facilities provided by the database.

Stand-alone users are the ones who use a database for their personal use and generally make use of some graphical user interface (GUI)-based interface or menu-based interface, for example, users storing their previous years' income tax details in a personalized database. These users become efficient in using a certain software package.

The people associated with a database are generally the ones who work on the scene, but the people associated behind the scene generally include **DBMS system designers and implementers, tool developers and operators, or maintenance people.**

A DBMS as a software package has to work on an operating system and thus requires an interface with it. **DBMS designers and implementers** are responsible for designing and implementing the various modules of the DBMS such as concurrency control, query processing, data recovery, data security, and catalog, which makes DBMS very complex software.

Tool developers develop tools, which are software packages used to facilitate the job of database modeling and design, performance monitoring, and test data generation. These tools don't come with the DBMS and are to be purchased separately.

Operator and maintenance personnel are responsible for actually running and maintaining the hardware and software needed to run the database successfully.

1.6.2 DBMS Services

The term database means collection of records, which when processed can be used for producing information.

The data stored in a database can be accessed, modified, managed, controlled, and organized to perform data-processing operations. There are different types of DBMSs, ranging from small systems running on personal computers to databases running on mainframes, for example, library systems, automated teller machines, flight/train reservation systems, and inventory systems (Figure 1.3).

A DBMS is a software that basically helps to access data stored in a database. The major components of a DBMS are as follows:

i. **Transaction Management**

Transaction is an operation performed on a database, and takes it from one state to another. Basically, transaction consists of a number of sequence of operations, which together form a logical unit. Transactions can update, delete, access, or modify a record. When a DBMS commits, the transaction is successful, and the changes made by the transaction are permanent, and if it fails, the system rolls back and brings the database to the original state. Transaction is discussed in detail in Chapter 8.

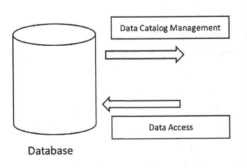

FIGURE 1.3   Services provided by DBMS.

ii. **Concurrency Control**

Since the database is shared between multiple users and applications, the operations performed can potentially interfere with each other and can lead the database to an inconsistent state. Concurrency control management service allows concurrency, that is, parallel access while maintaining the correctness of the data stored in the database.

iii. **Recovery Management**

Some of the transactions may fail. The recovery management mechanism ensures that these operations don't adversely affect the data stored in the database or other transactions. This mechanism of DBMS maintains the consistency of the data after a transaction fails or aborts. This mechanism works closely with concurrency control.

iv. **Security Management**

Unauthorized users should not be able to access the data in a database. Security management ensures this. The level of access privileges and operation to be performed or associated with a user account are closely watched by a DBMS.

v. **Language Interface**

Manipulation and accessing of the database requires some support languages. We have data definition language (DDL), data manipulation language (DML), and data control language (DCL). DDL deals with schemas and descriptions of the database, DML deals with data manipulation in the database, and DCL is mainly concerned with rights, permissions, and other controls of the database system. The language interface provided by database management software makes it easy for the users to do their jobs without looking into the details of database's physical implementation.

vi. **Storage Management**

Storage management of a DBMS manages the permanent storage of the data. We have three schemas for a database. Schemas define various views for the database. An external schema defines a view or views of the database for various users. A conceptual schema describes the structures of the data in a database. An internal schema defines how data is physically stored by the storage management mechanism and how the storage manager interfaces with the operating system to access the physical storage [10].

vii. **Data Catalog Management**

Data catalog also called metadata or data dictionary has the descriptions of the data being stored in a database such as relationships between data, constraints, and entire schema. Data catalog or dictionary is basically queried to get information for the structure of the database.

1.7 DATABASE CHARACTERISTICS

Managing information is one of the challenges that are met by using a DBMS. The information collected in a database becomes easily accessible and integrated without any accidental disorganization. Database processing power allows it to manipulate the data it stores so that it can be sorted, matched, linked, aggregated, skip fields, calculate, arrange, etc. These databases can be linked to websites for capturing data such as registered users, personal address book in your email client, collection of word-processed documents, and airline reservations.

The characteristics of a database that differentiate it from file-based approach are as follows:

i. **Self-Describing**

Database system is self-describing in nature as it not only contains data but also metadata, which describes the data and relationships between the data stored in a database. This separation of data and information of data makes it separate from the traditional file system where definition of data is part of the application programs only.

ii. **Independence**

The structure of the data stored in a database is defined in a data structure stored separately in the system catalog instead of in the programs like in the file-based system. If changes are required in case of database, only the structure of the file needs to be changed, whereas the programs remain untouched. However, in file-based storage, programs that access the file need to be changed as well. This is called program-data independence.

iii. **Multiple Views**

Database supports multiple views. View is defined as a subset of a database, which is dedicated and defined as per the need of the users as it contains only that data which interests the user.

iv. **Sharing**

Data in a database is shared among different users and applications. Concurrency control strategies are used to ensure that the data being accessed by multiple users and applications is always correct, and its integrity is being maintained.

v. **Nonredundancy**

Generally, nonredundancy refers to the point that no two data items in the database should represent one same real-world entity. In a more descriptive way, it says that each data item should be stored only at one place in a database. However, redundancy still exists in databases to improve system performance, but this kind of redundancy is limited only to application programming and is as little as possible.

vi. **Integrity**

Integrity refers to the correctness of the data stored in a database. This is done by defining and enforcing constraints on the data items so that users enter only valid information in the database. Constraints are basically rules that define what can be entered in a particular field in a database. For example, the postal code column/attribute in the database should be of a particular range or of a particular digit size. Data type defines the type of permitted data. Data uniqueness such as primary key ensures that the data entered in the column or attribute, which acts as the primary key, should be unique for each tuple/row, should not be null too, etc. Constraints can be simple or complex too (programming).

vii. **Security**

Data in a database is protected from unauthorized users. All the users of a database may not have the same privileges as they have different roles and responsibilities. It may be possible that one of the users may require read-only access, i.e., the ability to only read the content but not modify or update it, and some may require read and write privileges, which provides the ability to read, modify, and update the data in the database. Thus, in a database system, there must exist a control to provide different access rights to different user accounts and hence control unauthorized access too.

viii. **Persistence**

Persistence refers to the existence of the data in the database beyond the scope of the process that might have created it, i.e., it exists permanently in the database. The data stored is never lost until the data is not deleted explicitly. Even if a system failure occurs in between the transaction, the transaction will be rolled back or may be fully completed, but the data will never be at risk.

ix. **Consistency**

Consistency means whenever a program tries to update the data in the database, the real purpose of the data should not be lost. The values in the database should be consistent with respect to the relationship and constraints. This is achieved with the help of ACID properties.

x. **Backup and Recovery**

A database may also fail, resulting in loss of all the information and a big loss to the organization owning it. It is backed up at regular intervals in order to avoid such catastrophes. Backup and recovery is the characteristic of a database that makes it more effective too.

xi. **Any Kind of Data**

A database should be capable of storing any kind of data. It should not be capable of storing only employee id, name, salary, etc. but anything that can represent a real-world entity.

1.8 ADVANTAGES OF A DATABASE

1.8.1 Reducing Redundancy

In traditional systems, users are responsible for maintaining the files that are to be used by them for data-processing applications. For example, an accounts department of the university and examination department of the university would be having their own files for student names and enrolment numbers. Thus, these files will be a part of two user accounts, creating redundancy of data and wastage of storage space. Now if any record needs to be updated, it causes duplication of efforts at each end; sometimes, it may also lead to inconsistency of data, if data is not updated well in time in all files.

Database prevents this as there is single storage being shared among multiple users; so any change made is reflected immediately reducing the degree of efforts too.

1.8.2 Preventing Unauthorized Access

As discussed previously in Section 1.6.1, databases are shared between multiple users and applications. Different users may have got different roles in an organization, which allow them to access a particular kind of data in a database. For example, an employee of an organization won't be allowed to access the financial data of the organization. Databases allow only the authorized users to access the data, thus maintaining data security too. Users and user groups are given account numbers and passwords. The security and authorization subsystem of the DBMS is responsible for maintaining data security.

1.8.3 Faster Data Access

A database provides various storage structures and query optimization techniques for faster retrieval of data. It is stored on disk, and thus efficient search techniques such as indexes are supported. Indexes basically use tree data structures or hash data structures to quicken the disk access process. Also, DBMS provides buffering and caching, which maintain some data from the database in the main memory or cache. Query processing and optimization is also one of the strategies/techniques being followed to quicken the access process. There can be multiple queries that can be used to access data from a database, but the query processing and optimization module of DBMS helps in choosing the most efficient query execution plan.

1.8.4 Backup and Recovery

This advantage of databases has already been introduced in the previous section. The users are not responsible for backing up the database. The DBMS backup and recovery module backs up the data in a database periodically, i.e., at regular intervals to avoid the problems arising through catastrophic disk failures. Recovery module also ensures to bring the data to a consistent state in case of failure of a transaction or to start a transaction from the point where it was interrupted. In a nutshell, this module is responsible for recovering a database from software and hardware failures.

1.8.5 Multiple User Interfaces

As discussed in Section 1.6.1 there are different categories of users that may need an access to a database. These actors use the database in different ways and also have different technical abilities. So, it becomes very important to provide a variety of interfaces to different categories of users. This may include query languages for casual users, programming languages interfaces for application developers, and natural language interfaces for standalone users. The interfaces may be menu-driven GUI based or form-styled ones.

1.8.6 Enforcing Integrity Constraints and Support Inferencing/Actions

The data constraints ensure that the data being stored in a database is correct and meets the constraints. Constraints include integrity constraints, which must hold for the data being stored, one of them being the data type or the constraint which can limit the number of characters or values in the data item, etc. We have referential integrity constraint, key constraint, etc. as part of the database. Referential integrity constraint says that every record in a table should be related to other records in other tables, and key constraint ensures the uniqueness of the data stored. For larger applications, we have what are called to be business rules, which ensure that the correct data is being inserted in the specific columns. Inherent rules are the implicit rules of a database and are basically related to the data models used.

Inferencing and decision-making is what information is supposed to be used for. For inferencing, special databases called deductive databases provide rules, whereas in the traditional databases, this is done with the help of procedural programs [11]. For relational databases, triggers associated with tables are activated according to the rule specified and may perform some additional operations. Stored procedures are also used in databases for enforcing rules.

1.8.7 Persistent Storage

As discussed in Section 1.5, one of the main characteristics of a database is persistence that the data remains in the database until it is explicitly deleted. Databases provide persistent storage for objects and data structures. Generally, in programming languages, we have complex data structures like class definitions in Java and C++. Data and data structures are lost as soon the application program using them finishes or terminates. They are saved only when they are explicitly written to some file where they can be stored permanently. But this also requires converting these structures to the form which is file-compatible and vice versa. Object-oriented databases are highly suitable for such scenarios. They provide the compatibility between database data types and object-oriented programming languages.

1.8.8 Additional Benefits

In addition to the advantages discussed above, databases are capable of representing complex relationships between data items easily, reducing application development time, providing flexibility by bringing the change in the structure of data easily and economies of scale by reducing wasteful overlapping of activities of data personnel.

1.9 LIMITATIONS OF DATABASES

Despite the various advantages of databases discussed in the previous section, databases have some limitations too, which are listed as follows [12].

1.9.1 Increased Cost

There is an increase in cost associated with hardware and software component, staff training, and also data conversion since databases require a hardware system having powerful processors and memory sizes and also sophisticated software for managing such hardware. In addition, it also includes the cost associated with their maintenance such as licensing, regulation compliances, and application development.

Staff like DBAs, application programmers, data entry operators, etc. who are responsible for maintaining the database require to be hired and given necessary training, which also adds to the cost. Converting our file system data to a database requires hiring of database designers who also need to be paid for it.

1.9.2 Complexity

All the large organizations prefer databases instead of the traditional file-based approach to store data because of their advantages, which we have already discussed in the previous sections. Database management software which provides almost all the facilities to maintain the data in the database is complex software because of the various services provided by it. All the actors involved in accessing the data stored in a database or maintaining the database should have good knowledge of this software, as incomplete and improper skills may lead to data loss or database failure.

1.9.3 Performance

Databases need to be fast as they may have to cater to the need of a number of users at the same time. They should provide maximum efficiency, which requires frequent updating of the components of DBMS to tackle new threats and follow security measures.

In addition to this aspect, databases may not give better results of small-scale firms as their traditional file system may cater to their need efficiently, and a database may show poor performance. Performance is one of the major factors that cannot be overlooked.

Thus, there may exist certain scenarios where databases may not be the better option. Some of them being the following [13]:

- Well-defined applications that are not going to change at all.

- Real-time application requirement scenarios where DBMS overhead may cause problems.

- No shared data required.

- Embedded systems that have got limited storage capacity.

Case Studies

There are many applications in the market running at large scale and making use of DBMSs. Some examples follow:

- **Telecom**, where the database is used to keep a record of the data that is being updated every millisecond. The telecom industry uses databases to maintain records of calls made, customer details, network usage, etc.

- **Banking Systems** use DBMS for maintaining customer information, tracking the day-to-day transactions, generating bank statements, etc.

- **Industries** maintain databases for manufacturing units, warehouses and distribution centers. These databases are used to keep records of the products in and out. For example, distribution centers are responsible for maintaining the records of items coming in the center and being delivered to customers.

- **Sales** departments store customer information, product information, and invoice details in the database.

- **Airline** industry requires databases for maintaining the records of reservations, flight schedules, etc.

- **Educational sector** such as schools and colleges requires the database to maintain its employee and student records. For employees, it may need the database to store employee details, attendance, payroll, etc. For students, it needs the database to store details on students' courses, exams, library, attendance, etc. This is a lot of data and the kind of data which is highly interrelated with each other, which cannot be maintained with file-based data management because of the various issues we have already discussed in Section 1.5.

- **E-commerce or online shopping** websites such as Amazon and Flipkart have a huge amount of data including the product details, addresses of the customers, credit card information, and relevant list of products as per the query entered by the customer. All of this requires a very efficient DBMS.

1.10 SUMMARY

In this chapter, we defined what data is and how information is a critical resource for today's competitive market. We gave a brief historical perspective on the evolution of database applications. A file-based data management system suffered from many issues such as redundancy of data, inconsistency, security, and integrity issues, which were solved by using database systems. A DBMS is a generalized software package for implementing and maintaining a computerized database. The database and software together form a database system. The various services provided by the DBMS, along with components of a database system, were discussed. We discussed about the various users/actors or workers associated with the database system. Finally, we conclude with the advantages and disadvantages of databases along with

1.11 REVIEW QUESTIONS

1. Describe the history of databases with phase-wise evaluation.

2. Differentiate between data and information with the help of an example.

3. How is information smartly used to make decisions in a business? Explain.

4. Describe information cycle with its advantages and disadvantages.

5. What do you mean by quality of information?

6. Explain the various stages of databases, and also discuss why we are using databases.

7. Define and discuss the components of a database and its uses.

8. Discuss the main characteristics of the database approach and how it differs from traditional file systems.

9. Explain the responsibilities of DBAs and database designers.

10. Discuss the roles and responsibilities of different types of database end users.

REFERENCES

1. D. Nofre, M. Priestley, and G. Alberts, "When Technology Became Language: The Origins of the Linguistic Conception of Computer Programming, 1950–1960," *Technology and Culture*, vol. 55, no. 1, pp. 40–75, 2014.
2. C. W. Bachman, "The Origin of the Integrated Data Store (IDS): The First Direct-Access DBMS," *IEEE Annals of the History of Computing*, vol. 31, no. 4, pp. 42–54, 2009, doi: 10.1109/MAHC.2009.110.
3. G. O'Regan, "History of Databases," *Introduction to the History of Computing*, Cham: Springer, pp. 275–283, 2016.
4. E. F. Codd, "A Relational Model of Data for Large Shared Data Banks," *Communications of the ACM*, vol. 13, no. 6, pp. 377–387, 1970.
5. B. W. Wade and D. D. Chamberlin, "IBM Relational Database Systems: The Early Years," *IEEE Annals of the History of Computing*, vol. 34, no. 4, pp. 38–48, 2012, doi: 10.1109/MAHC.2012.48.
6. P. P.-S. Chen, "The Entity-Relationship Model—Toward a Unified View of Data," *ACM Transactions on Database Systems*, vol. 1, no. 1, pp. 9–36, 1976.
7. "Relevant and Reliable Information - Decision Quality [Book]." [Online]. Available: https://www.oreilly.com/library/view/decision-quality/97811 19144670/c06.xhtml. [Accessed: 10-August-2020].
8. P. Mishra, "20 Incredible Facts About IRCTC That Will Blow Your Mind," RailRestro Blog - Food in Train, 15-May-2020. [Online]. Available: https://www.railrestro.com/blog/20-incredible-facts-about-irctc-that-will-blow-your-mind. [Accessed: 01-May-2020].
9. "Components of DBMS," Studytonight.com. [Online Available:]. https://www.studytonight.com/dbms/components-of-dbms.php. [Accessed: 02-May-2020].
10. A. Watt and N. Eng, *Database Design*, 2nd ed., Victoria, B.C.: BCcampus, 2014.
11. Z. Telnarová and M. Žáček, "Deductive Approaches in Database Systems," Central European Symposium on Thermophysics 2019 (CEST), 2019.
12. S. Sumanthi, "Overview of Database Management System," *Fundamentals of Relational Database Management Systems*, pp. 1–30, 2007.
13. R. Elmasri, "When Not to Use a DBMS," BrainKart. [Online]. Available: https://www.brainkart.com/article/When-Not-to-Use-a-DBMS_11396/. [Accessed: 03-May-2020].

CHAPTER 2

Data Models and Architecture of a DBMS

2.1 EVOLUTION OF DATA MODEL

Data model is defined as an architecture that organizes the various sections of data and manages how data elements are related to each other. The concept of data modeling came into existence during the 1960s when management of information system became popular [1]. The first phase in the development of data models came with the proposal of the file system data model, which was mainly used by IBM in its mainframe systems. An example of this data model is virtual storage access management.

Even though records could be managed easily in this data model, the data elements could not be related to each other. To overcome this problem, the second phase of the development of data models came into picture in the 1970s with the development of hierarchical and network data models [2]. While in the hierarchical data model, there was only one parent node to which all the other nodes were connected, the network data model provided many-to-many relationships. An example of hierarchical data model is the IBM Information Management System, and that of network data model is Integrated Database Management System (IDMS).

The shortcomings of hierarchical and network data models led to the third phase of data models' development, which gave rise to relational data model in the mid-1970s [3]. It supported relationship modeling and relational data modeling. Due to its cheap and complex query optimizers, this data model was used in the database systems of most industries and is

DOI: 10.1201/9780429282843-2

still in use. Oracle and MySQL are very good examples of relational data model. The fourth phase started from the mid-1980s and is still prevalent at present where object-oriented model and an extended version of relational database model was introduced which could support object and data warehousing [4]. Some examples of this data model are Versant, Oracle 10 g, etc.

But all these data models didn't provide proper management and organization of the unstructured data leading to the phase which is the recent data model type developed for the present and the nearing future. The XML data model is used to sort a huge amount of information in XML format. The users can even query the stored data by using XQuery and manage it in the desired format. The XML data model includes dbXML and Tamino.

The database evolution happened in five "waves":

- The first wave consisted of network and hierarchical data models and (in the 1990s) object-oriented DBMSs; and was used from 1960 to 1999 [2,4].

- After that, the relational wave was introduced with all of the SQL products (and a few non-SQL) around 1990. But this also started to lose its popularity from 2008 [5].

- The decision support or multidimensional wave was introduced which included online analytical processing and specialized DBMSs around 1990, and is used till today [5].

- The graph wave began with The Semantic Web Stack from the Worldwide Web Consortium in 1999, with property graphs appearing around 2008 [5].

- The NoSQL was invented in 2008 to manage and organize big data of the industries. NoSQL was developed by Facebook's open-source versions of Hive and Cassandra [5] (Figure 2.1).

It doesn't matter whatever database model is utilized. DBMSs are used to manage databases in the context of real-world applications. From an application standpoint, the various database models all strive toward the same goal: to make data storage and retrieval easier. The fundamental distinction between various database models or data models is how they represent various relationships and constraints among data items or elements. We discuss the following database models in detail in this chapter:

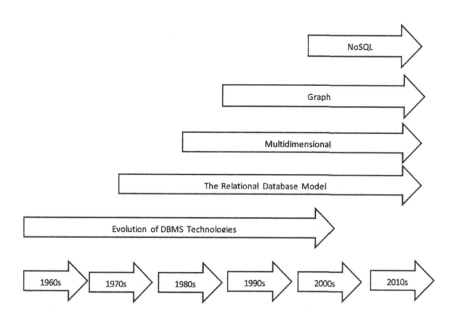

FIGURE 2.1   Data model evolution.

- Hierarchical database model

- Network database model

- Relational database model

- Object-oriented database model

- Object relational database model

2.2 HIERARCHICAL DATABASE MODEL

Hierarchical database model is one of the oldest database model in which data is arranged in a tree-like structure as shown in Figure 2.2. In this type of database model, data is stored as records, and they are connected through links with each other. Record is basically a grouping of fields, which contains or refers to one particular data item.

In hierarchical database model, there is only one parent node through which many child nodes are connected. Parent node can also be called the root node. In this model, multiple parent nodes are not allowed. In order to retrieve data from the hierarchical database model, we need to traverse the whole tree starting from the root node or the parent node. This model represents the relations in the form of **Logical Adjacency** or **Logical Proximity** in a linearized tree [6].

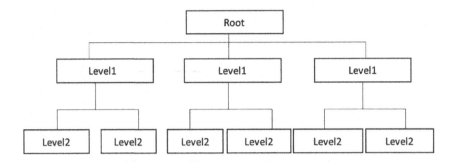

FIGURE 2.2   Hierarchical database model.

This can be understood with the help of an example. Let's take an example of a university. At the top, we will be having vice chancellor. Under him, we will be having multiple deans. Each dean looking after multiple departments. Each department will be having a head of the department and multiple employees under him. Separate rows will be used to represent the VC and each dean, each department, each HOD, and each employee in the hierarchical model. A connection between rows is implied by the row position. An employee is assigned to the department directly above it on the list, and the department is assigned to the HOD immediately above it, and so on.

This type of model is also known as one-to-many relationship model, which can be explained by taking two tables A and B. If each record in table A is linked with different records of table B, but each record in table B has only one linked record in table A, it is known as one-to-many relationship in hierarchical database model.

Hierarchical database model was used in the era of mainframe computers. In today's era, it can be used in applications which require high performance and availability like banking and telecommunications. Also, it can be used for storing file systems and the geographic information. This type of database model can also be used for the Windows Registry in the Microsoft Windows Operating System.

2.2.1 Advantages

There are many advantages of using hierarchical database model over file-based system which it replaced. Some of them are listed as follows:

- **Simple**: This model is very easy to understand as it follows the hierarchy, and also, it clearly depicts the relationship among different data items/layers logically.

- **Efficiency**: It offers better performance. Because parent-child connections may be constructed using pointers from one data to another, it is relatively quick. As a result, after discovering the first record, there is no need to go back to the index and look for another. It is highly suitable when a database requires one-to-many relationships and a large number of transactions. Also, in hierarchical database model, the parent and child records are stored very close to each other in a storage device, which minimizes the hard disk input and output.

- **Security**: This database model was the first model to introduce data security. It provided referential integrity, which means that it doesn't need to update each and every node; if the parent node is updated, it automatically updates the child node.

- **Integrity**: In hierarchical database model, there are links present between the table structures, which results in the fast access of data. Also, there is always a link between parent and child segment, thus promoting data integrity.

2.2.2 Disadvantages

Besides advantages, there are many disadvantages of hierarchical database model as well. Some of them are as follows:

- **Implementation Complexity**: Though hierarchical database model is simple to understand and design, the implementation of such database model requires good knowledge of physical characteristics of storage, and hence, it's very complex to implement.

- **Lack of Structural Independence**: This model uses the physical access paths in storage to reach the data segment. If the physical structure changes, the application will require to be modified. Thus, there is lack of structural independence. In a nutshell, we can say that this model has a rigid structure, which means that if we want to add a field to the existing record, we cannot do that by altering table command like in the sql database; in this scenario, we'll need to reframe the table for the bigger entries, and we'll need to create a new database structure if we want to add new relationships.

- **Programming Complexity**: Here, the user as well as the programmer has to be aware of how data on the storage is being accessed due to structural dependence of this model. Understanding the complex intricacies of the pointer system is just beyond the capability of a user of a database.

- **Implementation Limitation**: This model is not able to represent the many-to-many relationships, which are much common in real life.

2.3 NETWORK DATA MODEL

Charles Bachman created the network data model in 1969 to address the shortcomings of the hierarchical data model [7]. The hierarchical model has only one parent node, which is connected to all the other child nodes, whereas the network data model follows "many-to-many" relationship. Instead of each child having one parent, the network data model allows each child to have more than one parent. This can be thought like this: an author can write several research papers, and a research paper can be written by several authors.

The network data model resembles an upside-down tree, with the branches representing member data linked to the parent node. Because the data segments are connected to one other, navigating is simple.

A relationship is a set in this paradigm, and each set contains two records: an owner record and a member record. In a hierarchical data architecture, the owner record is comparable to the parent node, whereas the member record is similar to the child. The main distinction is that under the network data model, a record can be a member of several sets, allowing for many-to-many connections to be supported.

The network data model has many applications, one of which can be to find the possible number of paths that can help in the chemical reaction between two compounds or what is the shortest or fastest path between two cities.

This data model is incorporated in various databases such as Integrated Data Store, IDMS, and Raima Database Manager to name a few (Figure 2.3).

This figure explains the network data model. Store has three child nodes – Customer, Manager, and Salesman. The node order has three parent nodes (i.e., Customer, Manager, and Salesman) showing many-to-many relationship.

2.3.1 Advantages

- **Conceptual Simplicity**: Any data model should be simple to design and use. The network model, like the hierarchical model, is theoretically basic and straightforward to construct.

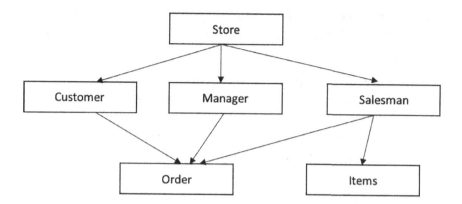

FIGURE 2.3   Network data model.

- **Capability to Handle Many-to-Many Relationships**: As stated above, the network model can help in finding the shortest and the longest path and even find different ways for the two compounds to react. Thus, this model can help in handling one-to-many and many-to-many relationships, which helps in real-life problems.

- **Ease of Access to Data**: Since this model is flexible, accessing of data becomes very convenient as all the information is linked unlike the hierarchical model. A set's owner record and member records can be accessed by an application. In reality, if it has many owners, it may be transferred from one to the next.

- **Data Integrity**: To prevent unwanted changes in the data, this model does not allow a member to access the data without the existence of the owner.

- **Data Independence**: The network model allows the isolation of the programs from the complicated physical storage details (partially not fully), which was earlier not possible in the hierarchical model.

2.3.2 Disadvantages

- **System Complexity**: Since all the data is stored and managed using pointers, the whole database structure becomes very complicated. The navigational data access mechanisms are very complex. Users along with database designers, administrators, and programmers should be familiar with the intricacies of data access mechanisms on storage leading to an unfriendly DBMS.

- **Operational Anomalies**: Performing operations such as insertion, deletion, and updation of the records/data requires a huge number of adjustments of the pointers.

- **Absence of Structural Independence**: As mentioned earlier in discussion of the network model, the structure is very complex, thus making structural changes to the database a very difficult task and sometimes impossible. Even if the changes to the database structures are made, it requires notification and modification of the application programs before accessing the data.

2.4 RELATIONAL DATABASE MODEL

Because of the disadvantages and complexities of implementation of hierarchical database and network database models, they were replaced by the relational database model. The relational database model can be accessed and managed by a special software called relational database management system (RDBMS). In this model, we have tables that represent the real-world entity in which data is arranged in the form of rows and columns. Structured query language (SQL) is used for maintaining and querying such databases.

Rows are also known as tuples or records, while columns are also known as attributes. Each table is related to only one entity, which is why it is known as a relational database model. Relational database model can be used in storing financial records, manufacturing products, personal information, etc.

2.4.1 Concepts of RDBMS

- **Tables**: Data is organized in rows and columns in a relational database format, and the table is made up of rows and columns.

- **Attributes**: Attributes are defined as the columns in the table which are basically a property to define a relation.

- **Tuple**: Tuple is defined as the single row in a table, which only contains a single record.

- **Relational Schema**: It is defined as the name of the relation with its attributes.

- **Degree**: Degree is defined as the total number of attributes in a relation.

- **Cardinality**: Cardinality is defined as the total number of rows in a table.

- **Column**: Column is defined as the set of values for a specific attribute.

- **Relation Instance**: It is defined as the finite set of tuples in the RDBMS.

- **Relational Key**: In each and every row, there are multiple attributes known as the relational key.

- **Attribute Domain**: It is defined as the predefined value or scope that every attribute has.

In the relational database model, the database can be altered using special operators some of which are insert, delete, etc.

Figure 2.4 clearly depicts the relationship between different entities. There are two tables named student and course, and each table has two attributes. For student table, we have Roll No and Name, and for course table, we have CID and Title. These tables are linked with Enrolled relationship. Marks and Joining Date are the two attributes of Enrolled.

Although the relational database model is the most often used, there are other database models such as object-oriented and deductive database models that are more flexible in data representation and better suited for commercial use.

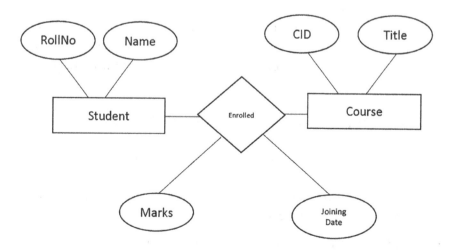

FIGURE 2.4   Relational data model.

2.4.2 Advantages

- **Conceptual Simplicity**: Although both the hierarchical and network database models were basic, the relational database model is considerably easier to use since the data is organized in the form of rows and columns, making it easy for users to alter the data.

- **Query Capability**: It is very user-friendly because it uses simple commands for the execution of queries which can be easily understood by any user. SQL used for maintaining and querying such database makes the ad hoc queries a reality here.

- **Structural Independence**: This database type allows you to modify the database without impacting the DBMS's ability to access data. As a result, database developers, engineers, and even end users are freed from having to learn about storage for navigational data access techniques.

- **Other Benefits**: In this model, different users can work easily at the same time because it prevents the traffic between the users by providing a separate layer for different users and also gives privacy for updation and modification. In this type of database model, admin can easily manage the users and authenticate the users to work on the database, and also the admin has the right to limit the rights of the users on the database.

2.4.3 Disadvantages

The disadvantages of a relational database model are very less in comparison to the advantages they provide. Moreover, the drawbacks can be avoided by taking proper corrective measures. Some of the disadvantages are listed below:

- **Bad Design**: Relational database is easy to be designed and doesn't require the designers to know about the storage details. This ease sometimes may lead to bad design also. Though these things don't come to picture when the amount of data stored is small, but as the size of data increases, poor database design leads to poor performance of the database too.

- **Information Isolation**: A relational database model is very easy to implement as we have already discussed. Due to the ease in implementation of this model, people and departments create their own databases and applications, which cannot be integrated together as would have been in a normal scenario where this would be necessary for an organization's seamless and effective operation. So many databases created in turn affect the very purpose of having a database. This would lead to data inconsistency, data duplication, data redundancy, etc.

- **High-Ended Hardware Requirements**: The ease of design this model provides also requires some overhead in hardware. This data model requires powerful hardware – computers and storage devices, which no longer is a big issue as the devices already are high-ended ones.

2.5 OBJECT-ORIENTED DATA MODEL

A relational database model no doubt being most easy to implement and also being popular cannot handle the complex information systems as it requires the application developer to enforce information model into table whose relationships are defined by values. Object database model is different as the database design here is the most important process of the overall application design process.

In an object-oriented data model, the data is stored in the form of objects. These objects can be thought of as the instances of the class and it is through these that we can access the class. These classes and objects together make an object-oriented model. This data model helps in the representation of real-world objects. It isolates each object from each other. This model has various features such as the following:

- **Object and Object Identifier**: Any real-world entity is modeled as an object in the same way.

- **Attributes and Methods**: A state and a behavior are properties of every object. Only through message passing through methods can an object's state and behavior be accessed/called from outside the entity.

- **Class**: It's a container for all objects with the same properties and functions. An abstract data type is analogous to a class.

- **Data Encapsulation**: This feature helps in the wrapping up of the data in a single unit. This single unit is called a class and no other object of other class can access this data except the inherited classes, thus preventing alteration of data by unauthorized users.

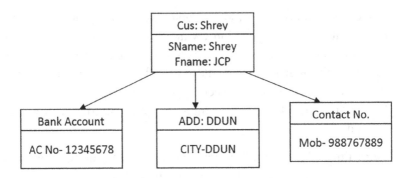

FIGURE 2.5   Object-oriented data model.

- **Inheritance**: Another feature of this model is that it's not necessary to write multiple codes for the same function. Through inheritance, the characteristics of one class can be inherited by the characteristics of another class, thus saving extra time and effort.

The object data model arose from research into having inherent database management support for graph-structured objects in the early to mid-1970s [8].

Figure 2.5 shows an example of multiple inheritance in which the customer class is inheriting properties from three other classes namely Bank Account, Address, and Contact Number.

2.5.1 Advantages

- **Object-Oriented Features**: Object-oriented features used in this database model enhance the productivity. Inheritance helps in reutilization of the codes, thus reducing the cost and effort to manage the same data multiple times. Polymorphism and dynamic binding also ease the job. One operation related to an object is defined, and then the specifications can be shared with other objects too. Dynamic binding makes sure at the runtime which operation has to be executed with the object depending upon the class of the object. Since this information is encapsulated inside the objects isolated from other objects, it prevents the data from being misused or altered. Encapsulation also helps to store all the information in a single unit, thus providing easy access to the data. All these features combined together provide ease to the database application developers.

- **Handling Different Data Types**: All the database models covered till now in this chapter, i.e., hierarchical, network, and relational data models have limitation on the different types of data they can handle. But the object-oriented data model can store any type of data such as audio, video, and pictures also.

- **Combination of Database Technology and Object-Oriented Programming**: Combining the object-oriented programming and database technology provides many benefits, e.g., including the operation definitions with data definitions makes these operations available across all the database applications and not limited to one. Complex data types, such as multimedia, can be added to the data types. This is accomplished by establishing object classes with operations that support such data.

- **Data Access Performance**: This database model supports navigational as well as associative access to information which is made possible by representing the relationships explicitly, which also results in better data access performance.

2.5.2 Disadvantages

- **Difficult to Maintain**: The data model represents the real world, as real world is not static, and so is this data model. The definitions of the objects may change, and the database may need to be migrated to match the new definitions. Schema migration is one of the biggest challenges. Simply migrating the data representation is not enough; it also requires the change in behavioral code for each object.

- **Application Suitability**: This model is not suitable for all kind of applications. They perform well in e commerce, engineering product data management, and special purpose database as in medicine and security.

These database models aren't a threat to the relational database model as they are used for some specific category of market where they are more suitable like in case of high volume and complexity data.

2.6 OBJECT RELATIONAL DATA MODEL

Object relational database can be defined as the combination of both relational database and object-oriented database. This database model can also be known as the Object Relational Database Management Systems (ORDBMS). This database model supports all the properties of object-oriented programming like objects, classes, inheritance, etc. and supports data types and tabular structures like relational database.

In a traditional relational database model, a developer only has limited data types for creation of a database, whereas in modern object relational data model, developers can develop their own data types for creation of a database. That's why object relational data model allows developers to increase the abstraction with which they view the problem area.

After a lot of research on different database models, researchers in the early 1990s came up with the idea of object relational database, which solves problems like complexity in the traditional relational database model [9].

This database paradigm allows tuple attributes to have more complicated kinds, such as non-atomic values or nested relations.

2.6.1 Advantages

There are many advantages of an object relational database model:

- **Complex Data Types**: In most SQL object relational database models, complex data generation is dependent on the user-specified data type's early schema design. Object relational database model allows its users to declare datatypes, functions, and operators. This results in increased performance and functionality of this database model.

- **Inheritance**: In object relational database model, users can inherit the properties of the objects, tables, etc. There are new attributes as well as the existing attributes in the inherited objects.

- **Method Encapsulation**: Procedures or functions that may be wrapped within an already established object are referred to as methods. This can be done to guarantee that programs can utilize the type of object's attributes to execute actions. Methods also describe how objects of that type behave.

- **Polymorphism**: With this technique, we can involve one operator which can have different meanings within the database. This technique can also be used to join tables within a database by building relationships among them.

- **Extensibility**: This data model is the extended version of a relational database model as it also supports the properties of object-oriented database model. This capability may be achieved by combining complicated data types with advanced object-oriented principles like inheritance and encapsulation.

The main advantage of this model is reuse and sharing, which means that this data model has the ability to extend the database management server to perform standard functions centrally instead of coded in each application.

2.6.2 Disadvantages

- **Complexity**: The primary downside of the object relational database architecture is its complexity; as previously said, it is a hybrid of relational and object-oriented databases. Because of object-oriented characteristics that are rather difficult to master, the simplicity and purity of the relational data model is lost in this data model.

- **Costly**: The other disadvantage is the cost. In object relational database model, the cost is very high as compared with the traditional relational database model.

Figure 2.6 presents the entity relationship in which a customer phone number attribute can have a value of 0–10. The customer's address may also be thought of as a single address object with multiple characteristics

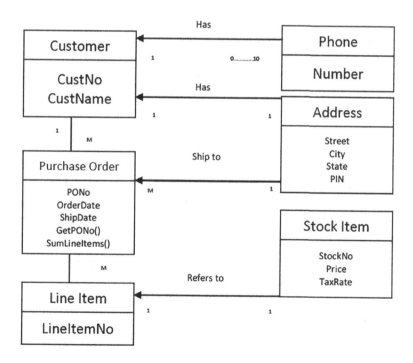

FIGURE 2.6   Object relational data model.

such as street, city, state, and zip code. Any purchase order objects that are connected with that customer can utilize the address object that is linked with that customer. An attribute of a purchase order is a collection of one or more line items, and each line item denotes one stock item.

2.7 THREE-LEVEL ARCHITECTURE OF A DATABASE

As we have already discussed in Chapter 1, a database consists of mainly four elements:

2.7.1 Data, Relationships, Constraints, and Schema

Data is the binary information of the logical entities represented in some special way. Along with data, software generally have what are called programs. Programs are a collection of instructions that are used to manipulate this data. *Relationships* represent the way how these data elements correspond to each other. The data stored in the database at any instance is called data instance or snapshot. *Constraints* are the predicates which ensure that the database is in the valid or correct state or not. When we say *valid state*, it means that the current data in the database satisfies the structure and constraints that are specified for schema. *Schema* basically describes the organization of the data and relationships within the data. In fact, in other words, we can say that schema represents the description of the database which is usually specified at the time of database design and doesn't changes frequently. For example, let's say for a student table, we may have Student ID, Name, Class, and Course as its attributes. This is the schema for a student table maybe in a college database. Whenever a new database is defined, schema is the first thing to be specified. Initially, the database is an empty state, i.e., it has no data. Then it is loaded with data to get into what is called as initial state. From then, the data will be updated frequently, and state will go on changing, and at any point of the time, the database state is called the current state. Two common terminologies used for schema and state are intension and extension, respectively (Figure 2.7).

The architecture of the most commercial DBMSs is mostly based on a single database architecture – ANSI-SPARC architecture [10].

This architecture comprises three levels, namely:

- Internal level
- Conceptual level
- External level

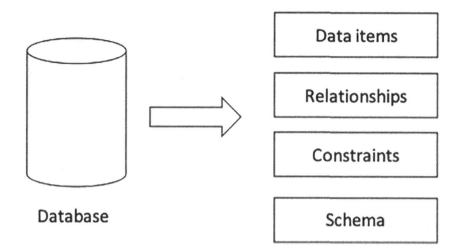

FIGURE 2.7   Components of a database.

These three levels provide data abstraction, i.e., they show only relevant information to the users while hiding the background details.

The main purpose of the database is that it should be efficient and convenient to use. To provide efficiency to the database, complex structures can be used at the internal level and simpler convenient interfaces at the external level. This can only be done using the three levels described as follows.

2.7.2 Internal Level

The internal level, also known as the physical level, is used to offer information on how data is saved in storage devices, as well as an interior look at the data that is physically stored.

Internal level works at the lowest level of data abstraction and deals with the complex low-level data structures, file structure, and access methods in detail. It also helps in data compression and encryption techniques.

2.7.3 Conceptual Level

Conceptual level is also called **logical level** and describes what type of data is stored in the database and how these elements are linked to each other. This level basically defines the stored data structures in terms of the data model used. The conceptual level of data abstraction is the next level up from the internal level. It also hides the actual storage's low-level complexity. Database administrators and designers work at the conceptual level to determine what sort of data should be maintained in the database.

2.7.4 External Level

External level is known as **view level**. It only refers to the section of the database that the end user is interested in. The external level is the most abstract level of data abstraction. This level allows users to access only the parts of the database that they need, rather than the full database, which saves time. Because various users have distinct database requirements, there can be a variety of view-level abstractions of the database.

Figure 2.8 describes the three levels of a database system. **Physical level**, which is directly attached to the database and has the records of what all information is being stored in the database, **Conceptual level**, which manages what type of data is stored in the database and how the data elements are related to each other, and **External level**, which helps the user to view only the part of the database that is important to them instead of the entire database. As shown in Figure 2.8, there can be more than one users who can view the database through external level.

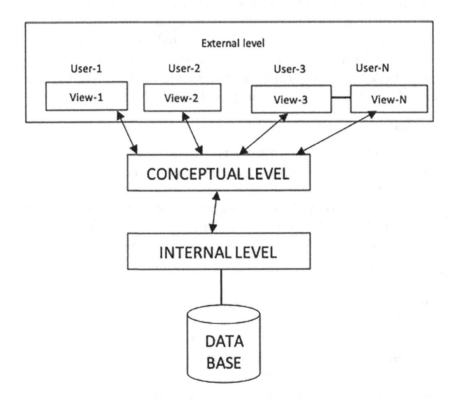

FIGURE 2.8   Three-level architecture of a database.

At each level represented in Figure 2.8, mapping is done from one level to another level. Mappings basically represent the conversion of requests and results from one level to another level. For example, at the external schema level, the user may have different views. These view requests need to be converted to the representation at the conceptual level and then to internal or physical level. Similarly, the data extracted from the database need to be presented back to the user, which again requires reformatting of the information according to different levels back to the external level.

2.7.5 Advantages

• The main advantage of these three levels is that they provide data abstraction.

• The user is unconcerned with the actual data storage specifics, and the same data may be accessed in a customized manner by multiple users.

2.8 DATA INDEPENDENCE

There are three levels of database as discussed in the previous section:

Internal Level: Internal level consists of a lower level of data abstraction and is basically physical storage of the database. It explains how the data is kept in the database and how the database uses data structures.

Conceptual Level: Conceptual level is a higher level of data abstraction than the internal level, and it describes the types of entries that are kept in the database and how they are connected to one another. This level contains the whole database's logical structure.

External Level: This level helps to view the content of the database that the user wants and not the entire database. A database has a single physical level and a conceptual level but has more than one external level according to the needs of the users.

Data independence is a DBMS characteristic that allows you to alter the database schema at one level of the database system without changing the schema at the next level. This function also aids in the separation of data from other applications. In addition to data in the database, a database stores data. This data is known as metadata, i.e., data about data. Also, it would be rather difficult to change metadata once it is stored in the database. But once the database extends, the metadata needs to be modified in order to meet the requirements of the user. If the entire data is dependent, it would be difficult to change the metadata. Also, the metadata follows the layered architecture, so when we change data, it does not affect the data at the other layer. The three-schema/level architecture discussed in the previous section helps us to explain the concept of data independence. Data independence is defined with the help of two concepts:

- **Logical Data Independence**: Logical data can be defined as the data about the database, which means that it stores all the information about how data is managed in the database. The capacity to modify the conceptual schema without impacting the external schema is referred to as logical data independence. Changing the conceptual schema here means deleting a record, inserting more records, changing the constraints, etc. This only will require changing the view definition and the mappings. Application programs that refer to the external schema don't undergo any change even after the logical reorganization.

- **Physical Data Independence**: It refers to the power to change the physical schema without changing the conceptual schema or logical data. Hence, the external schema also doesn't change. The internal schema may be changed when the files on storage devices are reorganized or faster access strategies are applied by providing new access paths.

Physical data independence is most common as file environments do hide the details of the exact location of data on storage, compression, and encoding techniques along with the splitting and merging of records [11]. These details are usually hidden from users, and also, applications are unaware of these details. Logical data independence is much difficult to be achieved in comparison to physical data independence as it requires application programs to be unchanged even when structural or constraint changes occur. The data independence at both the levels is achieved because of the change in the mappings. As a result, applications that refer to the highest-level schema do not need to be modified. The two-level mappings that must be changed in order to achieve full data independence, however, incur an overhead during query execution, resulting in performance inefficiencies.

2.8.1 Importance of Database Independence

1. It helps to improve the quality of the data that is being presented to the user.

2. Maintenance costs of the database system becomes inexpensive.

3. It also helps to secure the data by improving the database security.

4. To improve the performance of the system, easy modifications can be made in the physical level.

5. If any part of the system gets damaged, it helps to improve the state of that part in the system.

2.9 DATABASE LANGUAGES

Database languages are the languages that are crucial to express database queries and updates. These languages play a major role to read, update, and store data in the database. There are basically four types of database languages [12] (Figure 2.9).

Data Definition Language (DDL): DDL is made up of different SQL commands that are being used to design the database schema. This language acts like any other programming language in which the developer gives the input and gets the desired output. Some of the commands that are in DDL are listed below:

- CREATE is used to create table and objects.

- DROP is used to remove items from a table.

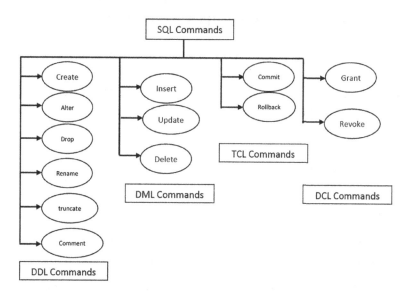

FIGURE 2.9 Database languages.

- ALTER is used to change the structure of a database.

- TRUNCATE is used to delete all records from the table, including all of the records' allotted spaces.

- The COMMENTS function is used to add comments to the data dictionary.

- RENAME is used to rename existing database items.

Data Manipulation Language (DML): DML consists of various SQL commands and can be used to manipulate or alter data in the database. Some of the commands that are in DML are listed below:

- The INSERT command is used to insert data into a database.

- The UPDATE command is used to update existing data in the database.

- The DELETE command is used to delete records from a database table.

   DML is further subdivided into high-level or nonprocedural DML and low-level or procedural DML. High-level or nonprocedural DML can be input interactively through a terminal to interact with DBMS, or it can be incorporated within a general-purpose programming language. Low-level or procedural DML, on the other hand, must be contained within a general-purpose programming language.

Transaction Control Language (TCL): TCL is used to manage different types of transactions in the database. Each transaction in a database begins with a particular task and ends when all the tasks are completed successfully. This language also manages the operations performed by DML. This language performs many tasks such as:

- COMMIT is used to save all the transactions in a database.

- ROLLBACK is used to restore the last transaction when there will be an error in the new transaction.

- SAVEPOINT is used to temporarily store the transaction so that a user can easily roll back to the transaction.

- SET TRANSACTION is used to set parameters for the transaction to occur.

Data Control Language (DCL): DCL is basically used to grant permissions to the users so that they can perform various operations on the database. It basically deals with the right and control of the database system. Some of the commands that are used in this language are listed below:

- GRANT is used to give permission to the users so that they can perform various read and write operations on the database system.

- REVOKE is used to take access back from the users. It basically cancels the permission that is granted to the user.

2.10 SUMMARY

In this chapter, we discussed in detail about the evolution of database models. We also discussed about the various database models like hierarchical, network, relational, object-oriented, and object relational. We saw an overview, advantages, and disadvantages of each model. We introduced three levels of database architecture in this chapter. The three levels were as follows: internal schema level, which specifies the database's storage structure, conceptual schema level, which provides a high-level description of the database, and external level, which defines the perspectives for users. We also discussed that this model supports the concept of data independence: logical and physical data independence. We also discussed the different types of database languages: DDL, DML, TCL, and DCL.

2.11 REVIEW QUESTIONS

1. Discuss the hierarchical database model.

2. Differentiate between hierarchical and network database models with the help of an example.

3. Relational database model is the most widely used database. Justify this statement.

4. List the advantages of using object-oriented database model over relational model.

5. Object relational database model is more secure than relational model. Explain.

6. Compare and contrast different database models.

7. Differentiate between a database schema and a database state.

8. Describe the three-schema architecture. Why do we need mappings between schema levels? How do different schema definition languages support this architecture?

9. Discuss and analyze logical data independence and physical data independence. Which one is harder to achieve? Why?

REFERENCES

1. K. L. Berg, T. Seymour, and R. Goel, "History of Databases," *International Journal of Management & Information Systems (IJMIS)*, vol. 17, no. 1, pp. 29–36, 2012.
2. K. D. Foote, "A Brief History of Data Modeling," Dataversity, 30-May-2017. [Online]. Available: https://www.dataversity.net/brief-history-data-modeling/. [Accessed: 05-May-2020].
3. D. Yatsenko, E. Y. Walker, and A. S. Tolias, "Datajoint: A Simpler Relational Data Model," arXiv preprint arXiv:1807.11104, 2018.
4. V. Singh, "Software Professionals use Object Oriented Data Modeling Instead of Traditional Relational Data Modeling," *International Journal of Advance Research and Innovation*, vol. 5, no. 3, 2017.
5. T. Frisendal, "History of Data Models and Databases," Graph Data Modeling. [Online]. Available: http://graphdatamodeling.com/GraphDataModeling/History.html. [Accessed: 06-May-2021].
6. "TYPES OF DATABASE MANAGEMENT SYSTEMS in IBM Mainframe Tutorial 21 June 2021- Learn TYPES OF DATABASE MANAGEMENT SYSTEMS in IBM Mainframe Tutorial (13827): Wisdom Jobs India," Wisdom Jobs. [Online]. Available: https://www.wisdomjobs.com/e--university/ibm-mainframe-tutorial-464/types-of-database-management-systems-13827.html. [Accessed: 06-May-2020].
7. T. Haigh, "Charles W. Bachman: Database Software Pioneer," *IEEE Annals of the History of Computing*, vol. 33, no. 4, pp. 70–80, 2011, doi: 10.1109/MAHC.2011.68.
8. M. Lade and V. Shinde, "Current and Future Trends of Database," *International Journal for Scientific Research & Development*, vol. 4, no. 2, 2016.
9. C. D. Tupper, "Object and Object/Relational Databases," *Data Architecture*, pp. 369–383, 2011.
10. T. Brinda and T. Terjung, "A Database Is Like a Dresser with Lots of Sorted Drawers," Proceedings of the 12th Workshop on Primary and Secondary Computing Education, 2017.
11. R. Elmasri, "Three-Schema Architecture and Data Independence," BrainKart. [Online]. Available: https://www.brainkart.com/article/Three-Schema-Architecture-and-Data-Independence_11399/. [Accessed: 07-May-2020].
12. D. V. Kumar, G. Raheja, and S. Singh, "Review of Database and Prominent Programmes," *International Journal of Computers & Technology*, vol. 4, no. 1, pp. 48–53, 2013.

CHAPTER 3

Relational Database Management System

The relational database management system is one of the major data models of database management systems where data is stored in the tabular form or we can say in the form of row and columns. In a RDBMS, a user can create, modify, and alter the database and manage the database. This model is widely used in the database applications.

The data is stored in the row and column called record and attributes, respectively. The data stored in tables allowed to be manipulated using database languages such as relational algebra with the help of relational operators in **relational database management systems**. Query language is used for adding, deleting, and manipulating data in a RDBMS.

3.1 DIFFERENCE BETWEEN RDBMS AND DBMS

1. RDBMS stores data in a tabular arrangement, whereas DBMS stores data as files.

2. RDBMS shows the relationships between the multiple tables, whereas in DBMS, there is no such kind of relationships.

3. RDBMS shows the dependency and normalization of the data.

4. RDBMS supports the distributed database processing.

DOI: 10.1201/9780429282843-3

3.2 FEATURES OF RDBMS

RDBMS supports various features, which makes it easy and convenient to be easily understandable to the users.

1. Data is stored in the row and column, due to which we get the results in less time and less number of iterations, which reduces the complexity.

2. In RDBMS, we can store the data without any duplicate records with the help of a primary key that also helps us to uniquely identify the data in the database.

3. We can create the views and indexes in RDBMS, which helps to secure and store the data easily.

4. We can achieve the different types of integrity in RDBMS as follows:

   a. *Entity Integrity*: No duplicate records exist in the table.

   b. *Domain Integrity*: All the records should have the valid entries as per its type and size.

   c. *Referential Integrity*: It will ensure that deletion and addition of records are done only with the permission of the parent relation.

   d. *Not-Null Integrity*: Any attribute can be defined as not-null, so it means the value for this will be mandatory for each records.

5. Multiple users can access the same database with the help of multiple views.

3.3 ADVANTAGES OF RDBMS

The state-of-the-art features of this relational model have more than justified its potential. However, in order to fully appreciate its utility, a brief description of its benefits is needed.

1. Since data is only stored once, frequent record changes are not necessary. Data deletion and alteration are also simplified, and storage performance is extremely high.

2. The Structure Query Language can be used to perform complex queries. Keywords in SQL such as "Insert", "Update", "Delete", "Create", and "Drop" assist in accessing a specific data set.

3. The creation of tables provides increased protection. This system will cover specific tables. Users may create access barriers to restrict who has access to what content is available. It is particularly useful in businesses where a manager can choose which information is shared with employees and customers. As a result, a personalized level of data security can be allowed.

4. Future criteria will be met because new data can be easily added and appended to existing tables, and the content can be made compatible with what was previously available. No flat file database has this capability.

3.4 DISADVANTAGES OF RDBMS [1]

Like there are two sides to a coin, a RDBMS houses a few drawbacks as well.

a. The cost of implementation is a downside of this successful scheme. A special piece of software is needed to set up a relational database management system. Data setup is a time-consuming process after it has been purchased. Millions of lines of text would need to be moved to the tables. In some cases, a programmer and a team of data entry experts are needed. At the time of data entry, care must be taken to ensure that secure data does not fall into the wrong hands.

b. Simple text data can be inserted and appended with ease. Newer types of data, on the other hand, may be perplexing. Complex pictures, figures, and designs are difficult to categorize into tables, which poses a challenge.

c. Another disadvantage is the structure's limitations. There is a character limit in some table fields.

d. If large pieces of data are segregated from one another, isolated databases can be established. It is not easy to link such large amounts of data.

3.5 EXAMPLES OF RDBMS

3.5.1 MySQL

MySQL is the most widely used open-source database on the planet. MySQL is the database backend for many of the web applications you can come across online, and it is used extensively by tech luminaries such as Facebook, Twitter, and YouTube.

3.5.1.1 Limitations for SQL Database

Users must scale relational databases on powerful servers, which are costly and difficult to manage. The database should be stored in the multiple servers for scaling the data, but it is difficult to manage these number of tables in different sites.

3.5.2 NoSQL

NoSQL termed as "not limited to SQL". In NoSQL, we can store and manage the unstructured data without schema in the multiple nodes that does not require the fixed table structure, and due to limited support of join queries, we can scale up in high amounts.

3.5.2.1 Benefits and Scope

3.5.2.1.1 Scalability   RDBMS (relational database management system) databases will scale vertically. As the load on an RDBMS database grows, we scale it by increasing server hardware capacity, which necessitates the purchase of more costly and larger servers, while NoSQL databases are built to scale horizontally and indefinitely. Horizontal scaling refers to expanding the pool of resources by adding more computers.

3.5.2.1.2 Less Expensive   Maintaining high-end RDBMS systems is costly, because database management requires qualified personnel, while NoSQL databases need less management. Many features, such as automatic repair, easier data delivery, and simpler data models, reduce the amount of administration and tuning required in NoSQL.

3.5.2.1.3 Cost-Effective and Open-Source   NoSQL databases are low-cost and free to use. RDBMS databases are costly and require large servers and storage systems, while NoSql databases are simple to implement and usually use inexpensive servers to handle the exploding data and transactions. As a result, the cost of storing and processing data per gigabyte in NoSQL can be several times lower than in RDBMS.

3.5.2.1.4 No Schema Definition   Data may be loaded into a NoSQL database without any predefined schema since it is schema-less. As a result, the format or data model may be modified at any time without affecting the program. In SQL, change management is a big headache.

3.5.2.2 Disadvantage and Limitations

As NoSQL is an open-source database, its greatest advantage is it has limited establishment requirement.

GUI mode database access tools are not widely available in the market, and finding nosql experts is difficult.

3.5.3 PostgreSQL

In recent past, PostgreSQL becomes very much popular due to its open-source nature. Although it is not as widely used or common as MySQL, its developers take pride in adhering to industry standards and adhering to the ANSI-SQL:2008 standard.

PostgreSQL is available for most operating systems, including BSD, Linux, MacOS, Solaris, and even Windows. It is also becoming more widely available on all levels of hosting packages, avoiding the need to install by ourselves.

3.5.4 Microsoft SQL Server

Microsoft has been promoting its SQL Azure cloud storage service, but it is still difficult to ignore SQL Server, the stalwart old RDBMS workhorse.

You can get a free trial version, a complete free Developer edition, or the smaller Express edition to get yourself up and running on Linux, Docker, and MacOS in addition to Windows.

While commercial licenses are still more expensive than open-source alternatives such as MySQL and PostgreSQL, there is little doubt about the power and quality of the associated tools such as Management Studio, SSIS, SSAS, and SSRS.

3.6 RDBMS TERMINOLOGIES

RDBMS terminology include Database, Table, rows, Columns, etc.

Database: Database is a collection of tables like <Student>, <Teacher>, etc.

Table: A table is a collection of rows and columns, for example, Student.

Roll No.	Student_Name	SapId
R001	Tom	1
R002	David	2
R003	John	3

Row: It is a collection of values for all applicable attributes; it is also called tuple.

Row-1	R0001	Jagdish	Dehradun	Clement Town	965647456
Row-2	R0002	Ravi	Dehradun	Chaman Vihar	987654556

Column: A column consists the values of all the records

Roll No.	Name
R0001	Jagdish
R0002	Ravi

3.7 KEYS IN DATABASE [2]

3.7.1 Super Keys

Each record in a table is uniquely identified by a collection of one or more columns (attributes) known as a super key. A super set of candidate keys is referred to as a super key.

Roll No.	Name	City	Street	Mobile No.
R0001	Jagdish	Dehradun	Clement Town	965647456
R0002	Ravi	Dehardun	Chaman Vihar	987654556

In the student table given above, Roll No. is unique in relation. This can be selected as a super key. Also, we can select more than one column as a super key to uniquely identify a row, like (Roll No., Name), (Roll No., City), etc.

3.7.2 Candidate Keys

A candidate key is a set of one or more columns (attributes) that uniquely identifies each record in a table, but the selected attribute must not contain redundant values (cell repetition). A subset of the super key is candidate key.

Roll No.	Name	City	Street	Mobile No.
R0001	Jagdish	Dehradun	Clement Town	965647456
R0002	Ravi	Dehardun	Chaman Vihar	987654556

Here, student relation Roll No. is a unique attribute. Roll No. can be selected as candidate key. We can also select other combinations as candidate key those can uniquely identify a record from the relation. We can take any column as a part of candidate; those are not having repeating values like City.

3.7.3 Primary Keys

Primary keys are used to uniquely identify a record in relation. It is compulsory to have a primary key in every table to uniquely identify the relation; otherwise, it will be referred to as a weak relation. All the candidate keys are eligible to become the primary key, but whatever key selected by the programmer in the database as key is called as primary key.

Roll No.	Name	City	Street	Mobile No.
R0001	Jagdish	Dehradun	Clement Town	965647456
R0002	Ravi	Dehardun	Chaman Vihar	987654556

Primary Key

Roll No. attribute can uniquely identify the records in the table given above, so it is going to be the primary key for the abovementioned relation.

3.7.4 Composite Keys

A composite key has at least two or more than two attributes used to uniquely identify the records in a relation; in the abovementioned relation, Roll No. and Street are combined to uniquely identify the record in relation.

3.7.5 Secondary or Alternative Key

The attributes other than part of primary key is called as secondary or alternative keys.

Example: If we consider Roll No. and Street as primary key, then Name, City, and Mobile No. are called as secondary or alternate keys.

3.7.6 Foreign Keys

Branch	
BranchName	Branchcity
Bidholi	Dehradun
Premnagar	Dehradun

It is an attribute in one table that refers to the primary key of any other table. It has a relationship with the primary key in another table.

Account	
AccNo	BranchName
101	Bidholi
102	Premnagar

In the abovementioned example, Account and Branch are two relations where AccNo is the primary key in Account relation and BranchName is the primary key in Branch relation. Here, BranchName is acting as a foreign key for Account relation that refers to the primary key of Branch relation. The records at Account relation will only be validated if it is confirmed from branch relation.

3.7.7 Difference between Primary Key, Candidate Key, Super Key, and Foreign Key

Primary Key	Candidate Key	Super Key	Foreign Key
This ensures the unique value for each and every record in the relation.	Candidate specifies the key which can qualify for primary key.	This is an attribute or set of attributes used to uniquely identify the records from a relation.	This is an attribute or group of attributes in a table by which we can link the multiple tables.
A relation will have maximum one primary key.	A relation can have more than one candidate keys.	A relation can form multiple super keys, and from these keys, we can select the candidate keys.	A relation can have more than one foreign keys.
It does not allow NULL values.	In the candidate key, any attribute can contain NULL value.	Super key's attributes can contain NULL values.	It can also contain NULL values.
It is the minimal set of attributes that are required to uniquely identify the records in a relation.	This is the subset of super key that can be used to uniquely identify the records.	Super Key can be any set that is used to uniquely identify the records from a relation.	An attribute referring to other relation is called the foreign key and the referred attribute should be primary key in another relation.

3.8 INTEGRITY CONSTRAINTS IN DBMS

Only approved users may change the database, and data accuracy is ensured by integrity constraints. At the time of schema definition, integrity constraints are established. The constraints are defined in SQL DDL commands such as 'create table' and 'alter table'.

Any time the database is modified, the database system checks the required constraint. Any update that modifies the database while also violating an integrity restriction is refused. Every time a database is modified, the authorization and integrity manager tests the integrity restriction [3].

3.8.1 Integrity Constraints

a. Entity Integrity

b. Referential Integrity

c. Domain Constraints

d. Assertion

3.8.1.1 Entity Integrity Constraints
The entity integrity restriction guarantees that a relation's primary main attribute does not contain a null value. Since the primary main attribute value uniquely identifies an object in a relation, this is the case.

It is not important to specify that every attribute in a relation is not-null when declaring it as the primary key attribute. The special main constraint is part of the entity honesty constraint.

Create table Student

(Roll_no varchar (5), name varchar (20) not null, depart_name varchar (20), Primary Key (Student_id));

The candidate key is made up of the set of attributes marked as special. In a relation, no two entities (tuples) must have the same value for the candidate key attribute. Unless they are explicitly declared to be "not null," candidate main attributes will accept "null" values.

3.8.1.2 Referential Integrity Constraints
The values for a set of attributes in one relation must appear the same for the same set of attributes in another relation, according to referential integrity. The same attribute or attributes of other relations are referred to by the attribute or set of attributes of one relation.

Consider the following student relationship:

Account (Acc_No, Branch_Name, Balance)
Branch (Branch_name, Branchcity)

In this example of account relation, it has an attribute, Branch_name, that is having the details of all the accounts details at different branches, and in the branch relation, branch_name is also an attribute that is the primary key.

Now, it is important that no accounts are possible without a branch, but branches can exist without accounts (that happens when the branch is newly opened or going to close). The abovementioned statement means that branch will act as parent relations, whereas account will act as child relation.

In the above example, while we are doing any kind of manipulation at account relation, we have to make sure that there should be a branch existing of the same name in the branch relation.

Here, we are referring to the values of *Branchname* from account relation to branch relation for validation; this concept is known as referential integrity.

The concept of referential integrity is achieved by foreign key keyword in the database declaration.

create table *branch*
(Branch_name **varchar (20),** *Branchcity* **varchar (20) not null,**
primary key *(Branch_name),*
);
create table *Account*
(Acc_no **varchar (5),** *Branch_name* **varchar (20) not null,** *balance int,*
primary key *(Acc_no),*
foreign key*(Branch_name)* **references** *Branch*
);

The foreign key attribute should be the primary key in the parent relation, which means Branch_name attribute should be the primary key in Branch relation. It is important to ensure that the value we are denoting in child relation should be present in the parent relation; otherwise, it will be the violation of referential integrity and the record is going to be rejected. It is like inserting a tuple in the account relation with the Branch_name value that does not exist in the Branch_name attribute of some tuple in Branch relation.

3.8.1.3 Domain Constraints

A domain restriction guarantees that an attribute's value is justified by its domain. When we declare some database reference, we define a specific domain for each attribute when we declare its attribute.

The domain of an attribute defines all of the values that can be assigned to it. Declaring the domain of an attribute serves as a restriction on that attribute, defining the range of possible values.

> create table *Account*
> (*Acc_no* **varchar (5)**, *Branch_name* **varchar (20) not null**, *balance int*,
> **primary key** *(Acc_no)*,
> **foreign key***(Branch_name)* **references** *Branch*
>);

In the abovementioned example, the balance attribute of account relation can only accept integer values of variable length; it cannot accept character values or a date or time value.

Other domain constraints are

    a. Not null constraint

    b. default constraint

    c. check clause constraint

3.8.1.4 Not Null Constraint

Null is the legal value for all the attributes that are specified in the definition of SQL. If an attribute has NULL value, it means either the value is not applicable or not known. Rest of the attributes will have the values that need to be entered.

In the abovementioned account relation, the branch_name attribute is specified by not null, so it means that the value for branch_name cannot be null. So it is important to specify the not-null while declaring the schema.

Once we declare the attribute as Not Null, it means we are restricting the attribute to accept the values and in the absence of values, the record is not going to be accepted.

An example of not null is explained in the following example.

> create table *Account*
> (*Acc_no* **varchar (5)**, *Branch_name* **varchar (20) not null**, *balance int*,

primary key *(Acc_no),*
foreign key*(Branch_name)* **references** *Branch*
);

In SQL, **primary key attribute by default has the not null property,** which means the primary key attribute should always have a value.

3.8.1.5 Default Value Constraint
With the help of these constraints, we set the default value for an attribute. If we do not have values for such attributes where we specify the default constraints, it will insert the specified default values for the same.

For example:

```
create table Account
(Acc_no varchar (5), Branch_name varchar (20) not
null, balance int default 0,
primary key (Acc_no),
foreign key(Branch_name) references Branch
) ;
```

In the abovementioned example, we have set the default value 0 for the balance; so in the case of no value for balance, it will automatically insert the value 0 as per default statement.

3.8.1.6 Check Clause
This will ensure that a relation should satisfy the given predicate specified in the check clause. If the values are as per the check clause, then it will be inserted otherwise it will be rejected.

```
create table Account
(Acc no varchar (5), Branch_name varchar (20) not
null, balance int),
primary key (Acc_no),
Check (Acc_no like 'IND%'),
foreign key(Branch_name) references Branch
) ;
```

As per the check clause in the abovementioned example, it ensures that every account number should always start with "IND". If we are adding a record and its account number value is not starting with "IND", then the record will be rejected, as it is not satisfying the predicated mentioned in the abovementioned example.

3.9 RELATIONAL ALGEBRA

The procedural query language RELATIONAL ALGEBRA is commonly used. It takes relation instances as input and returns relation occurrences as output. This action is carried out using a variety of operations [4]. Recursive relational algebra operations are performed on a relation. These operations produce a new relation, which can be made up of one or more input relations [5].

Relational algebra operations are basically divided in two categories: unary and binary.

3.9.1 Unary Operators

- Select
- Project
- Rename

3.9.2 Binary Operators

- Union
- Intersection
- Set Difference
- Cross Product
- Join
- Division

3.9.2.1 SELECT Operator

The SELECT operator is used to find the subsets of records that are satisfying the given predicate. Sigma (σ) is used to represent the select operator.

Sr. No.	Name	City	Marks
1.	Jagdish	Dehradun	45
2.	Ravi	Baraut	65
3.	Hitesh	Bijnor	52
4.	Avita	Jammu	76
5.	Tanupriya	Kolkata	42

Example: Find out the names of all those students whose marks are less than 50.

$\sigma_{marks<50}$(student)

This relational algebra expression will find out the tuples from student relation having marks less than 50.

Sr. No.	Name	City	Marks
1.	Jagdish	Dehradun	45
5.	Tanupriya	Kolkata	42

3.9.2.2 PROJECT Operator

It only displays those attributes defined in the projection and eliminates rest of the attributes. With this operator, we will get the subset that is vertically fragmented as per the attributes used with project operator.

This will eliminate the duplicates and display all the unique values for the projected attributes.

For example:

$\Pi_{Name, city}$ (students)

It will display the values for name and city attribute from the student relation.

Name	City
Jagdish	Dehradun
Ravi	Baraut
Hitesh	Bijnor
Avita	Jammu
Tanupriya	Kolkata

3.9.2.3 Union Operation

$\cup$ symbol is used for union operation. Let us take two relations A and B, then the union operator will have all the tuples from A and B and will eliminate the duplicates. It also eliminates duplicate tuples. It will be represented by $A \cup B$.

For a union, the following conditions must hold:

- Should have same number of attributes for union.

- The domains of the attributes should be compatible.

- Union operation will remove duplicates automatically.

Name	City	Marks
Jagdish	Dehradun	45
Ravi	Baraut	65
Hitesh	Bijnor	52
Avita	Jammu	76
Tanupriya	Kolkata	42

Relation-Student

Name	City	Marks
Priyanka	Dehradun	67
Ravi	Baraut	65
Shrey	Dehradun	78
Avita	Jammu	76
Parisha	Dehradun	89

Relation- Student1

Consider the two abovementioned relations and performing student union student1; that will give the following result.

Name	City	Marks
Jagdish	Dehradun	45
Ravi	Baraut	65
Hitesh	Bijnor	52
Avita	Jammu	76
Tanupriya	Kolkata	42
Priyanka	Dehradun	67
Shrey	Dehradun	78
Parisha	Dehradun	89

It includes all the tuples from student and student1 relation and eliminates the duplicate tuples.

In another example, let us find the all students names from student, student1 relation. The relation algebra expression for this will be

Π_{Name} (student) $\cup$ Π_{Name} (student1)

The result of the abovementioned expression will be

Name
Jagdish
Ravi
Hitesh
Avita
Tanupriya
Priyanka
Shrey
Parisha

3.9.2.4 Set Difference

Set difference operator is represented by a symbol -. A - B produces a relation that includes all tuples that are in A but not in B.

- The name of A's attribute must match the name of B's attribute.

- The two-operand relationships A and B must be compatible or Union compatible.

- It should be described as a relation made up of tuples that are in relation A but not in relation B.

For example, let us find the all students names that are in student relation but not in the student1 relation, so the relational algebra expression will be as follows.

Π_{Name} (student)$-\Pi_{Name}$ (student1)

Name
Jagdish
Hitesh
Tanupriya

3.9.2.5 Cartesian Product(X)

This operation can be used to combine columns from two different connections. In general, when a Cartesian product performs alone, it is never a significant operation. When it is supplemented by other activities, however, it takes on new meaning.

Name	City
Jagdish	Dehradun
Priyanka	Delhi

Employee

Mobile No.	Make
87665544	Ford
76767676	Maruti

Employee1

The result of cross join for the two abovementioned relations will be

Name	City	Mobile No.	Make
Jagdish	Dehradun	87665544	Ford
Jagdish	Dehradun	76767676	Maruti
Priyanka	Delhi	87665544	Ford
Priyanka	Delhi	76767676	Maruti

Employee X Employee1

3.9.2.6 Join Operations

The different types of joins are as follows:

e. Inner Join

As per the definitions of inner join, only those records are displayed that have satisfy the matching criteria and rest are going to be excluded.

f. Theta Join

It uses the predicate, and only those records are going to displayed that satisfy the given predicate.

A ⋈θ B

Let us take the following table into account.

Table A		Table B	
Attribute1	Attribute2	Attribute1	Attribute2
1	1	1	1
1	2	1	3

A ⋈ _{A.attribute2 > B.attrubute2} (B) will generate the following result

Attribute1	Attribute2
1	2

g. EQUI join

When we used equal sign while using the predicate, it is termed as equi join.

A ⋈ _{A.attribute2 = B.attrubute2} (B) will generate the following result when applied on the two abovementioned tables, A and B

Attribute1	Attribute2
1	1

h. NATURAL JOIN (⋈)

It can be only performed when joining relations have the common attributes. The attribute's name and form must be the same.

RollNo	Student Name
1	Jagdish
2	Ravi
3	Tanupriya

Stu1

RollNo	F_Name
1	Prayag
2	Rajkumar
4	Ramesh

Stu2

Stu1⋈stu2 will result in the following

Roll No.	Student Name	F_Name
1	Jagdish	Prayag
2	Ravi	Rajkumar

i. OUTER JOIN

Along with tuples that meet the matching criteria, we include any or all tuples that do not meet the criteria in an outer join.

3.9.3 Left Outer Join

The operation allows all tuples in the left connection to be held in the left outer join. If no matching tuple is found in the right relation, the right relation's attributes in the join result are filled with null values.

For example, stu1 left outer join stu2 will result as follows

Roll No.	Student Name	F_Name
1	Jagdish	Prayag
2	Ravi	Rajkumar
3	Tanupriya	NULL

Stu1 ⋈ stu2

3.9.4 Right Outer Join

The right outer join operation allows all tuples to remain in the correct relationship. If no matching tuple is found in the left relation, the attributes of the left relation are filled with null values in the join result [6].

Roll No.	Student Name	F_Name
1	Jagdish	Prayag
2	Ravi	Rajkumar
4	NULL	Ramesh

Stu1 ⋈ stu2

3.9.5 Full Outer Join

In a complete outer join, regardless of the matching condition, all tuples from both relations are included in the result.

Roll No.	Student Name	F_Name
1	Jagdish	Prayag
2	Ravi	Rajkumar
3	Tanupriya	NULL
4	NULL	Ramesh

Stu1 ⋈ stu2

3.10 STRUCTURED QUERY LANGUAGE (SQL)

The Structured Query Language (SQL) is a database language that allows you to update, delete, and request data from databases. SQL is the de facto mainstream database query language and is an ANSI and ISO standard. SQL is supported by a number of well-known database devices, including Oracle and Microsoft SQL Server. It is commonly used in both industry and academia and is often used for large amounts of money.

A software known as the database's "back end" runs continuously on a server in a distributed database system, viewing data files on the server as a traditional relational database. Users can manipulate data using tables, columns, rows, and fields in client computer programs. Server programs submit SQL statements to the server to accomplish this. SQL will be discussed in detail in Chapter 6 and PL/SQL will be discussed in Chapter 7.

3.10.1 SELECT Statements

A select statement retrieves the records from a database as per the given query.

Example 1.

Select name, city from student where marks>=50;

In the abovementioned example, it will display the value of name and city for those tuples whose marks values are greater than or equal to 50.

Example 2.

Select * from student where city=Dehradun;

In the abovementioned example, it will display all the tuples whose city name is Dehradun.

Example 3.

Select * from student where city like 'D%';

In the abovementioned example, it will display all the tuples whose city name starts with D.

SQL is not case-sensitive (for example, SELECT is the same as select).

3.11 CODD'S 12 RULES OF RELATIONAL DATABASE

E. F. Codd was a scientist who developed the relational database management model. The 12 rules of Codd describe the characteristics that a database management system must have in order to be classified as relational, i.e., a relational database management system.

Rule 0: Rule of thumb

Any system that claims to be a relational database management system must handle the data in a relational manner.

Rule 1: Information rule.

Tables with rows and columns are used to represent all data (including metadata). The rows and columns must be in a specific order.

Rule 2: Guaranteed entry.

A combination of table name, primary key, and column name should be able to access all values in a database. (According to this provision, the ability to access data directly using a pointed is invalid.)

Rule 3: Systematic Null values

In a database, NULL values may be used to reflect the absence of data or invalid data in a systematic way. Any operation on NULL values must return NULL regardless of the data type.

Rule 4: Online Catalog

A database's catalog is its full summary. It is accessible through the internet and provides additional database information. On the catalog, the query language used on the database is also used.

Rule 5: Well-Structured Language

Multiple languages can be supported by a relational database. However, at least one language should be able to perform all forms of data access, manipulation, and analysis. SQL is one such language.

Rule 6: View/Updation rule

The code should be able to update all views that are potentially updatable.

Rule 7: Quality Data Manipulation

Insertion, deletion, and updating should all be possible with a single operand. At all levels of relationships, this facility must be open.

Rule 8: Physical Data Independence

Physical improvements to the system, such as storage space changes, access methods changes, and so on, do not have an effect on the system's programs and other operations.

Rule 9: Logical Data Independence

Even if the logical structure of the relational database changes, the user view should remain consistent. This law is extremely difficult to follow.

Rule 10: Integrity Independence

Integrity constraints specific to a relational database should be specified and stored in the catalog in that database's language. This rule states that relational databases are not dependent on the front end.

Rule 11: Distribution Independence

Even if the database's data is spread over many sites, the end user can perceive it as a single entity. Furthermore, even though the database is spread throughout the network, it should function flawlessly.

Rule 12: Nonsubversion Rule

If a relational database has low-level access, it should not be able to alter data by circumventing integrity constraints and bypassing protection.

3.12 DATABASE DEVELOPMENT LIFE CYCLE

Database initial analysis, database design, installation and loading, testing and evaluation, running, and maintenance and evolution are the six phases of the Database Life Cycle (DBLC), as shown in Figure 3.1 below [7].

It is a collection of views or tables that give you access to database schema metadata, such as a list of tables, columns, and keys [8].

3.12.1 The Database Initial Study

The designer must analyze the current system's function inside the organization to assess how and why it fails in the database initial analysis. It consists of the following items:

- Analyze the scenario

- Define the problems and other constraints

- Objective's scope and boundaries

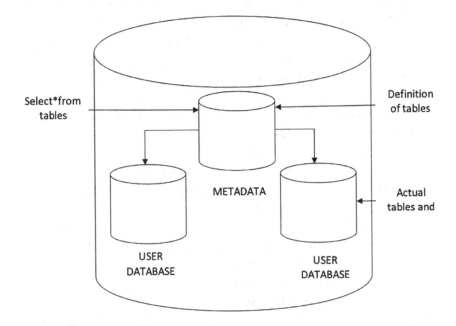

FIGURE 3.1   Database development life cycle.

3.12.1.1 Analyze the Scenario

The business situation defines the general operating conditions, organizational structure, and mission of a company. The database designer must figure out what the company's organizational components are, how they function, and how they communicate in order to assess the situation.

3.12.1.2 Define the Problems and Other Constraints

Both formal and informal sources of knowledge are available to the designer. The process of identifying problems can seem unstructured at first. End users are often unable to describe the broader nature of a company's operations or to recognize the real issues that arise during operations.

3.12.1.3 Objectives Scope and Boundaries

A proposed database system must be structured to assist in the resolution of at least one of the major issues discovered during the problem discovery process. In any case, the database designer must start thinking about the following issues:

What is the initial goal of the proposed system?

Will the device be able to communicate with other current or potential company systems?

Can the data be shared with other systems by the system?

The designer must understand that there are two types of limits: scope and boundaries. The complexity of the structure determines the size of the design based on organizational needs. Will the database design be for the whole company, one or more divisions within the company, or one or more departments' functions? Knowing the scope aids in the creation of the required data structures.

3.12.2 Database Design

The database model that will help the company's activities and goals is designed in the second phase. This is the most important step of the DBLC: ensuring that the final product meets user and device specifications [9]. Keep these points in mind as you review the procedures needed to complete the design process of the DBLC:

- The study and construction of a larger framework are closely linked to database design. The data variable is only one part of a larger data structure.

- The other system elements are designed by systems analysts or systems programmers. Their activities result in procedures that aid in the transformation of database data into useful knowledge.

3.12.3 Implementation of Databases

A set of instructions describing the development of tables, attributes, domains, views, indexes, security constraints, and storage and performance guidelines is the result of the database design process. During this process, you can actually put all of the design requirements into action.

3.12.3.1 Install the DBMS

This phase is only needed if the device requires a new dedicated instance of the database management system (DBMS). The DBMS may be built on either new or existing servers. Virtualization is a common trend right now. Virtualization is a method of generating logical representations of computing resources that are separate from the underlying physical resources.

3.12.3.2 Database Creation

A new database implementation in most modern relational DBMSs necessitates the construction of special storage-related structures to house the end-user tables. The storage group (or file groups), table spaces, and tables are the most common constructs.

3.12.3.3 Populate the Data

The data must be loaded into the database tables after the database has been developed. The data would most likely have to be transferred from an earlier version of the framework. Data for the system must frequently be gathered from various sources. Data from other databases, non-relational databases, flat files, legacy systems, or even manual paper-and-pencil systems which need to be imported.

3.12.4 Testing and Evaluation

Decisions were taken during the design process to ensure the database's integrity, stability, efficiency, and recoverability. These arrangements were in place during implementation and loading. The DBA checks and fine-tunes the database during testing and evaluation to ensure that it performs as intended. This process takes place in tandem with application programming.

3.12.4.1 Database Test

The DBA checks the database at this point to ensure that it retains the data's integrity and security. The DBMS ensures data integrity by enforcing primary and international key laws. Physical protection, password security, access rights, data encryption, and other factors must all be considered during database testing.

3.12.4.2 Tuning of Database

Database performance is normally one of the most critical factors in database implementation, despite the fact that there are no requirements for database performance steps. Different systems can put different demands on the database in terms of efficiency. The database's success on different tasks can be influenced by a variety of factors.

3.12.4.3 Database Evaluation

The system must be analyzed from a more holistic perspective as the database is developed and checked. Individual component evaluations can lead to a series of larger system tests to ensure that all of the components work together to meet the users' needs. Backup and recovery strategies are checked to ensure that the data in the database is safe against failure.

3.12.5 Operation

It can be used after the assessment phase is cleared. All the stockholders should complete all the information. After clearing the operation stage, the system will initiate the evaluation stage.

3.12.6 Maintenance of Database System

The database administrator must be ready to conduct database maintenance on a regular basis. Preventive maintenance is necessary:

Periodic maintenance activities (backup)

Maintenance that corrects a problem (recovery)

Maintenance that adapts to the situation (enhancing performance, adding entities and attributes, and so on).

Pass permissions are assigned and maintained for new and existing users.

3.13 SUMMARY

In this chapter, we have seen the difference between DBMS and relational DBMS and how the records are stored in the RDBMS. The records are represented in the form of row and column; rows are also known as records or tuple and columns are also known as attributes. In RDBMS, we define the various constraints like primary key, foreign key, etc. that are used for easy use of the database. Primary key is used to uniquely identify the records from a relation; while there can be many candidate keys in a relation, any one of the candidate key can work as primary key. To maintain the integrity between the other relations, we will use the referential integrity constraints that ensure that no manipulation will take place without verification of parent relation. Domain constraints also ensure that only specified values can be entered. Various relational algebra operators show how the queries are processed in the database.

Case Studies

HOSPITAL MANAGEMENT SYSTEM

The HMS program brings together all information about physicians, patients, nurses, hospital administration, and so on. It is made up of various sections that make up a hospital with different occupations. To begin, the system's key features and functions will be discussed. The system's primary users are then defined in terms of their positions and privileges. Finally, the database's entire work flow is defined.

Main Database

Login

This enables users to log into the HMS with their duties and privileges in mind. The user can access the system's functions and features after logging in.

Registration

This allows for the registration of new patients. Receptionists can use this to build accounts for new patients, and patients can then view their profiles.

Administrator

This is the master controller for the entire HMS device. Furthermore, this module is used to manipulate user information.

Patient

This regulates the flow of patients. It is used to register patients, obtain clinical information, display care, and monitor medical records and reports. In addition, it contains all of the patient's records, including their name, address, contact information, and date of birth.

Doctor

This is a list of physicians' names, as well as their schedules or appointments. It also contains a list of medications that are available for particular diseases, allowing the doctor to quickly look for an alternative if necessary. With reference to the doctor's schedule, an appointment may be made for the patient. HMS encourages and streamlines the coordination between doctors and patients in this way.

Nurse

This module has the details of nurses who are assigned to the doctors. It also includes the various tasks assigned to the nurses in regard to the patients.

Appointment

This will schedule a doctor's appointment in accordance with the patient's request. It assists in coordinating the availability of doctors at any time that is convenient. It establishes a new patient's appointment by identifying the doctor, time, date, and department that are available at the time. The patient is given an appointment based on the doctor's schedule.

Laboratory

The results of a specific patient's tests are displayed. When a doctor suggests a new set of tests, the HMS is revised, and the laboratory obtains the results (Assistant). This module is used by the lab assistant to analyze and document all of the specifics of the tests performed. The laboratory results are available to hospital personnel and can be used in medical records.

Pharmacy

This effectively controls inventory supplies and expiration dates. It allows HMS staff to keep track of medication stocks and warn concerned HMS staff when things run out of stock.

Billing

This attempts to list all of the patient's expenses at once and produce a full bill at the conclusion of the consultation (visit). This module can only be accessed by the cashier in order to produce patient bills. This saves time and effort because the hospital departments will no longer have to produce different bills.

The Main Users of HMS System

The main users of the HMS are as follows:

1. *Admin*: Admin has complete machine access, allowing him to manage any process-related operation. Admin is the most privileged user on the device, with full access to everything. He can make any improvements he wants, such as recruiting new doctors or HMS employees. He can also edit the profiles of all HMS users.

   Roles and functions:

   i. Manage HMS staff

   ii. Register new staff

   iii. Provide the resources

   iv. Monitor and prepare patient payments

   v. Ensure the availability of medicines in the hospital

   vi. Monitor laboratory and other diagnosis reports

2. Patient

   Roles and functions:

   i. Request new appointment

   ii. Modify previous appointment

   iii. Select the available doctor

   iv. Download and see the different reports

   v. Transaction history made for the various payment in the hospital

   vi. Feedback

   vii. Edit profile

3. ***Main Desk***: The main desk is the first point of contact for patients. They are in charge of registering new patients and updating their profiles as appropriate. They have access to the doctor's appointment schedule and can schedule an appointment as soon as a patient requires one.

Roles and functions:

i. Manage the appointments

ii. Schedule an appointment with respective doctor

iii. Registration of the patients

iv. Submission of registration and other fee

v. Provide unique ID

4. Doctor

Roles and functions:

i. Update patient details with symptoms

ii. Refer for diagnoses

iii. List of appointments

iv. View the nurse schedule

v. Generate prescription

vi. Examination results and its reports

vii. Own profile management

5. Nurse

Roles and functions:

i. Update patient records

ii. Primary health check ups

iii. Maintain doctors schedule

iv. Own profile management

v. Patient management as per availability of doctors

6. Lab Assistant specimens
   Roles and functions:

   i. Patient detail updating

   ii. Examination and its reports

   iii. Generate and print reports

   iv. Cost management of reports

   v. Profile management

7. Pharmacist
   Roles and functions:

   i. View Prescription

   ii. Medicines as per patient's prescription

   iii. Cost management

   iv. Update the stock

   v. Profile management

8. Cashier
   Roles and functions:

   i. Invoice management

   ii. Payment collection

   iii. Refund management

   iv. Transaction management

   v. Profile management

3.14 REVIEW QUESTIONS

1. Discuss the various features of an RDBMS.

2. Discuss and define different Codd's 12 rules for Relational Database.

3. Explain and differentiate among primary key, foreign key, candidate key, and super key.

4. Referential integrity is ensuring that no records can be entered without the permission of parent relation. Justify this statement with the help of an example.

5. Explain the unary operations in relational algebra with the help of an example.

6. Consider the following relational schema
   Employee (empno, name, office, age)
   Books (isbn, title, authors, publisher)
   Loan (empno, isbn, date)
   Write the following queries in relational algebra.

   a. Find the names of employees who have borrowed a book published by McGraw-Hill.

   b. Find the names of employees who have borrowed all books published by McGraw-Hill.

   c. Find the names of employees who have borrowed more than five different books published by McGraw-Hill.

   d. For each publisher, find the names of employees who have borrowed more than five books of that publisher.

7. List down the differences between MySQL and NoSQL in terms of implementation issues.

8. Explain the join operation. Differentiate between natural join and self-join with an example.

REFERENCES

1. Disadvantages of Database Systems (12 May 2021), Liberty University.
2. Keys in Database Management System (DBMS) (17 January 2021), https://www.includehelp.com/dbms/keys-in-database-management-system.aspx.
3. Integrity Constraints in DBMS (18 March 2021), https://binaryterms.com/integrity-constraints-in-dbms.html.
4. Paul Beynon-Davies, "Database Systems", https://doi.org/10.1007/978-0-230-00107-7.
5. Relational Algebra (27 May 2021), https://www.guru99.com/relational-algebra-dbms.html#6.
6. Outer Join (10 June 2021), Oxford University.
7. Database Development Life Cycle (18 April 2020) http://www.myreadingroom.co.in/notes-and-studymaterial/65-dbms/506-database-development-life-cycle.html.

8. The Database Life Cycle (11 February 2021), http://docshare04.docshare.tips/files/14097/140976542.pdf.

9. Database Design (28 January 2021), https://www.university.youth4work.com/bac_botswana-accountancy-college.

CHAPTER 4

Entity-Relationship Model

The relationship between entity sets is depicted in an entity-relationship (ER) model. An entity set is a collection of related entities having a set of attributes, but in some cases, an entity may not have the attributes [1]. In relational database management systems, a relation will have the set of records and the set of attributes that are depicted by a logical structure called ER diagram.

4.1 ER DIAGRAM

Student and college are two entity sets in the following ER diagram. stud-yIn is the relationship between these two entity sets and this is many-to-one as a college has many students, but a student cannot study in multiple colleges at a particular time. Stu_Id, Stu_Name, and Stu_Addr are the attributes form the student entity set, and col_Id and Col_name are the attributes for the college entity set (Figure 4.1).

Here in the ER diagram, the following notations are used

Rectangle: Entity sets.

Ellipses: Attributes

Diamonds: Relationship set

Lines: Link between one entity set to the relationship and between the entity set to the attributes.

Double Ellipses: Multivalued attributes

Dashed Ellipses: Derived attributes

DOI: 10.1201/9780429282843-4

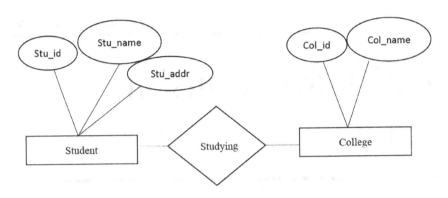

FIGURE 4.1   University ER diagram.

Double Rectangles: Weak entity sets
Double Lines: Total participation of an entity in a relationship set

4.2 COMPONENTS OF AN ER DIAGRAM

An ER diagram has three main components:

1. **Entity set**

2. **Attributes**

3. **Relationship**

4.2.1 Entity Set

An entity is a data object or component, and an entity set is a collection of similar entities. In an ER diagram, an entity set is represented by a rectangle. We have two entity sets in the following ER diagram: Student and College, and these two entity sets have a many-to-one relationship because many students attend a single college. There are two forms of entity sets: weak and strong [2] (Figure 4.2).

FIGURE 4.2   Entity sets.

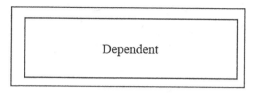

FIGURE 4.3   Weak entity set.

4.2.1.1 Weak Entity Set

Weak entity sets are those that can't be uniquely defined by their own attributes and depend on relationships with other entities. A double rectangle represents the weak entity set. A dependent, for example, cannot be individually defined without understanding which employee the dependent belongs to, making it a weak entity (Figure 4.3).

4.2.1.2 Strong Entity Set

An entity set uniquely identified by its own attributes is called a strong entity set. The strong entity set is represented by a rectangle, for example, a student relation uniquely identified by the attribute like roll no. as every student will have a unique value of roll no.

4.2.2 Attributes

It is represented as oval in the ER diagram and describes the property of an entity.

The following are the different types of attributes used in an ER diagram

   a. Key attribute

   b. Composite attribute

   c. Multivalued attribute

   d. Derived attribute

4.2.2.1 Key Attribute

A main attribute may be used to distinguish one entity from another in a group of entities. A student's roll number, for example, may be used to distinguish one student from another. The oval represents the key attribute, much like the other attributes, except that the text of the key attribute is underlined (Figure 4.4).

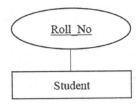

FIGURE 4.4 Key attribute.

4.2.2.2 Composite Attribute

A composite attribute is an attribute that is made up of several other attributes. The student address, for example, is a composite attribute in the student entity since an address is made up of other attributes such as street, town, and city (Figure 4.5).

4.2.2.3 Multivalued Attribute

The term "multivalued attribute" refers to an attribute that can hold several values. In an ER diagram, it is defined by double ovals. Mobile number, for example, is a multivalued attribute since a person can have multiple phone numbers (Figure 4.6).

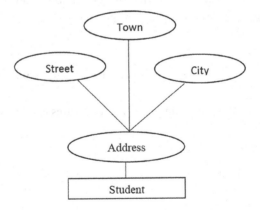

FIGURE 4.5 Composite attribute.

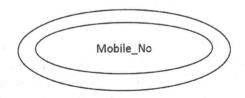

FIGURE 4.6 Multivalued attribute.

4.2.2.4 Derived Attribute

A derived attribute doesn't have its own value but can be obtained with the help of other attributes. Dashed oval is used to represent a derived attribute in the ER diagram. For example, age is a derived attribute, which can be obtained with the help of current date and date of birth.

4.2.3 Relationship

It is the relationship among the entity sets and is represented by diamond in the ER diagram. The types of relationships are as follows [3]:

    a. One-to-one

    b. One-to-many

    c. Many-to-one

    d. Many-to-many

4.2.3.1 One-to-One Relationship

A one-to-one relationship occurs when a single instance of one entity is linked to a single instance of another entity. For example, a man has only one wife, and a woman has one husband (Figure 4.7).

4.2.3.2 One-to-Many Relationship

A one-to-many relationship occurs when a single instance of one entity is linked to several instances of another entity. For example – a mother can have many children, but a child can have only one mother (Figure 4.8).

4.2.3.3 Many-to-One Relationship

A many-to-one relationship occurs when several instances of one entity are linked to a single instance of another entity. For example – many children can have only one mother, but a mother can have many children (Figure 4.9).

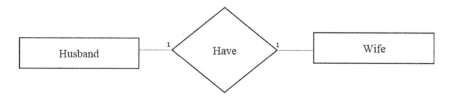

FIGURE 4.7   One-to-one relationship.

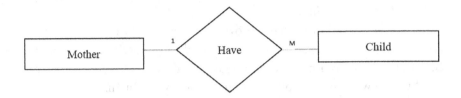

FIGURE 4.8   One-to-many relationship.

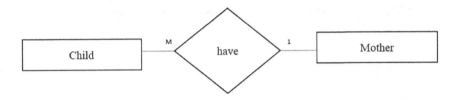

FIGURE 4.9   Many-to-one relationship.

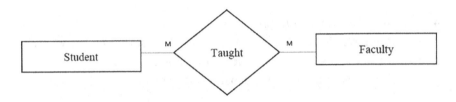

FIGURE 4.10   Many-to-many relationship.

4.2.3.4 Many-to-Many Relationship

A many-to-many relationship occurs when more than one instance of one entity is linked to several instances of another entity. For example, a student can be taught by many faculty members, and a faculty member can teach many students (Figure 4.10).

4.3 PARTICIPATION CONSTRAINTS

A strong entity may have a relationship with another strong entity, or a strong entity can have a relationship with a weak entity. Participation in the partnership may be partial or absolute, depending on the type of person involved. There are two forms of participation barriers to consider [4]:

- Partial participation
- Total participation

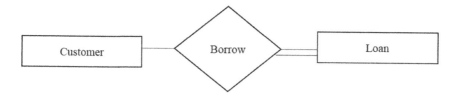

FIGURE 4.11 Participation constraints.

Partial Participation: If any of the entities of one entity type is not affiliated with one or more entities of another entity type, partial participation occurs. This is expressed by a single line entering the relationship with the entity form.

  Example: We have two entity types: "Customer" and "Loan". Then there can be "Customer" who has no Loan at any branch. So, here there is partial participation of the entity in the relationship that is shown by a single line (Figure 4.11).

  Total Participation: When all of an entity type's entities are linked to one or more of another entity type's entities, total participation occurs. This is expressed by a double parallel line connecting the relationship to the entity form. A strong entity and a weak entity normally have this kind of relationship. In the above ER diagram, every Loan has a Customer, so Loan is totally participating on the borrower relationship.

4.4 STRONG AND WEAK RELATIONSHIP

4.4.1 Strong Entity Set

A strong entity set is not dependent on any other entity set for unique identification of records. A strong entity will always have a primary key. Strong entities are represented by a single rectangle in the ER diagram. The relationship between two strong entity sets is represented by a single diamond. The relationship between two strong entity sets is known as strong relationship. In the following ER diagram, both student and faculty are strong entity sets as both have the key to uniquely identifying the records from the relation (Figure 4.12).

4.4.2 Weak Entity

A weak entity set is dependent on a strong entity to uniquely identify the records from a relation. Unlike a strong entity, a weak entity does not have any primary key. Weak entity sets have a discriminator key instead of a primary key for best identifying the records from a relation. A weak entity

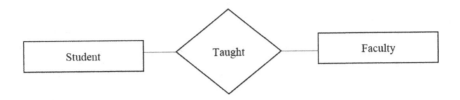

FIGURE 4.12   Strong relationship.

FIGURE 4.13   Weak relationship.

set is represented by a double rectangle. The relation between strong and weak entity sets is represented by a double diamond. The primary key for the weak entity set comprises the primary key of the strong entity set and the discriminator of the weak entity set (Figure 4.13).

In the above example, Customer is a strong entity set, whereas Loan is a weak entity set.

Customer – Strong entity set – represented by rectangle

Loan – weak entity set – represented by double rectangle

Borrower – relationship between strong and weak entity set – represented by double diamond

4.5 HANDLING MANY-TO-MANY RELATIONSHIP

- During the warehouse design process, the existence of many-to-many relationships adds complexity. Real-world examples of many-to-many relationships that need special consideration in the data model and schema are as follows [5]:

- Each salesperson in a company will operate in several call centers, and each call center has a large number of salespeople.

- A car manufacturing plant produces a variety of car types, each of which is available in a variety of colors. That is, a single type of car can come in a variety of colors, and several types of cars can be associated with the same color.

The following parts illustrate a many-to-many relationship using the illustration of objects and colors. One color can be associated with many items, such as red dresses, red caps, red shoes, and red socks, and one color can be associated with many items, such as red hats, blue hats, and green hats.

The following are two types of potential issues with many-to-many relationships, all of which can be avoided by correctly modeling the relationship [6].

a. Analytical capability

b. Multiple counting

4.5.1 Loss of Analytical Capability [7]

When it comes to the color and item many-to-many relationship, users normally have two business questions in mind:

- What colors are available for certain items?

- How many of a certain object or color combination is sold?

In order to answer the first question, you'll need a table with a list of all possible item/color combinations.

This is not possible in many-to-many relationships. Rather, the database must contain a separate relationship table. The look-up tables will be listed below:

Lookup color: Color_ID, Color_Desc

Lookup-Item: Item_ID, item_desc

And the relationship table will be Rel_Color_Item provides a row for every possible item/color combination.

Rel_Color_item: Color_ID, Item-ID

To answer the second question, you'll need a fact table with sales data, as well as color and object data. The tables below depict the same scenario as before, but they also include a simple fact table with sales data keyed by object, color, date, and sale_amt.

Lookup color: Color_ID, Color_Desc

Lookup-Item: Item_ID, item_desc

Rel_Color_item: Color_ID, Item-ID

Fact: Color_ID, Item-ID, Date, Sale_amt

To answer the first question, the table in the diagram above is insufficient. This table can only be used to retrieve items and color variations that were actually sold and therefore have sales records. This fact table cannot include a full list of item and color combinations to answer question one if we have items and color combinations that are available but have never been sold.

To summarize, the following conditions must be met to avoid any lack of analytical versatility when dealing with a many-to-many attribute relationship:

1. A separate relationship table to define all possible attribute element combinations between attributes.

2. In the fact table, both the attribute ID columns.

4.5.2 Multiple Counting

Loss of analytical capacity isn't the only issue when dealing with many-to-many relationships. Multiple counting is another major problem. If any of the following occurs, multiple counting occurs:

1. Aggregates the data of many-to-many relationship attributes.

2. The relationship is recorded in a separate relationship table.

3. The fact table does not include all of the attributes in the many-to-many relationship.

In the above example, make the following change: remove color from the fact table.

Fact: Item-ID, Date, Sale_amt

Assume there are three pieces total: hats, dresses, and socks. With the exception of socks, which are only available in green and blue, all pieces are available in three colors: red, blue, and green.

When you run a question demanding sales by color, you're essentially aggregating to the item attribute level in a many-to-many relationship, and you run the risk of multiple counting. Since color is not registered in the fact table, this question will require both the fact table and the relationship table.

The problem is that color isn't included in the fact table. There is no way to explicitly link the color of an object in the fact table to the sales of that item. Instead of measuring the sales of red products, the question, for example, aggregates sales for all red items according to the relationship table. Both hats and dresses, including blue and green ones, are included in the total. As a result, the figures for red goods are clearly higher than the actual sales.

The following questions cannot all be answered correctly using the information provided:

1. Amount of total sales for hats?

2. Amount of total sales for red items?

3. Amount of total sales for red dresses?

We may provide physical help using one of three methods to answer questions that can't be answered correctly using many-to-many relationships. Flexibility varies between the three strategies, and flexibility is often a trade-off with complexity. In any case, the two essential components are present in some form or another:

1. Defining of attribute relationship by a relationship table.

2. Attributes column in the fact table.

Additional data in the fact table is needed for the methods that follow. As a result, the additional data must be captured in the source system. For example, we need information about the color of each item sold in the source system. We can't completely overcome the many-to-many relationship to quantify the sum of revenue for products of a certain color if this additional data was never collected in the source system.

4.5.2.1 Method 1
This is the simplest approach for efficiently managing many-to-many relationships [7].

This necessitates the development of a separate relationship table (Rel_ Color_ Item in this case) and the addition of both attribute IDs to the fact table.
Lookup color: Color_ID, Color_Desc
Lookup-Item: Item_ID, item_desc
Rel_Color_item: Color_ID, Item-ID
Fact: Color_ID, Item-ID, Date, Sale_amt

4.5.2.2 Method 2

The many-to-many relationship and the need for a separate relationship table are eliminated with this process.

A compound attribute relationship is created by converting a many-to-many relationship into a compound attribute relationship. We treat one attribute as though it were a child of the other, and the lower level attribute has a compound key. Also, we add both attribute IDs, in this case, Item_ID and Color_ID, to the fact table as shown in the following diagram.

Lookup color: Color_ID, Color_Desc

Lookup-Item: Item_ID, Color_ID, item_desc

Fact: Color_ID, Item-ID, Date, Sale_amt

Although this approach removes the need for a separate relationship table, it also eliminates the right to display objects without regard to their color, or vice versa.

4.5.2.3 Method 3

It is the most adaptable option and includes the following features:

1. The compound attribute relationship from Method 2 is further simplified into a simple attribute relationship.

2. Allows you to display the object and color together or separately.

3. For full versatility, only one attribute column in the fact table is needed rather than two.

We will define a new attribute other than color and item that will have one-to-many relationship between itself and parent attributes. Here we have used the JCP attribute for this purpose.

Instead of including color and item, we will include the JCP attribute in the fact table. The same is represented in the following table.

Lookup color: Color_ID, Color_Desc

Lookup-Item: Item_ID, item_desc

lookuoJCP: color_ID, Item_ID, JCP_ID

Fact: JCP-ID, Date, Sale_amt

In fact, this method is very similar to Method 1. The main difference is that Method 1's distinct relationship table has an extra column, JCP, that combines the relationships of each item and color combination into a single value. As a result, this single value can be included in the fact table.

The main drawback of Method 3 is the time it takes to create a new attribute if your business model doesn't already have one, as well as the possibility of adding complexity to the ETL process.

4.6 EXAMPLE OF ER MODEL

4.6.1 An ER Diagram of an Organization (Figure 4.14)

a. Multiple departments

b. Name of the department, department number, department manager
   Manager is also an employee having starting date and locations of the department

c. Projects at the department
   Project name, project number, project location

d. Employee name, social security number, address, sex, salary, date of birth.

e. Employee will work for one department only but can work in multiple projects and number of hours spent on each project, employee supervisor details, dependent details with its attributes.

4.6.1.1 Initial Conceptual Design of the Company Database

First, we identify the entity types

Employee

Department

Project

Dependents

The attributes for each entity form are then determined. Multivalued attributes, composite attributes, derived attributes, and attributes with null values are all examples of multivalued attributes. Key characteristics are either known or suspected. For instance, we'll assume that each project has its own project number.

4.6.1.2 Relations and Its Structure

1. The entity sets participate in the relationship set, for example, employee and department participate by works_for as a relationship set.

2. Degree represents the number of entity sets that are participating in the relation set, for example, works_for having degree of 2 as two entity sets employee and departments are participating in works_for.

3. Recursive relationship means that an entity set is relating with itself like an employee can act as a supervisor.

4. A relationship set can have different cardinality rations like 1:1, 1:N, M:N.

5. Another constraint is participation, that is, how the entities of one entity set are participating in the relationship set. It can be total or partial; if all the entities are participating in the relationship set, then it is called total, otherwise it will be called partial.

4.6.1.3 Tables for Company Database
DEPARTMENT
(Name, Number, {Locations}, Manager, ManagerStartDate)
PROJECT
(Name, Number, Location, ControllingDepartment)
EMPLOYEE
(Name, SSN, Sex, Address, Salary, BirthDate, Department, Supervisor,
DEPENDENT
(Employee_no, DependentName, Sex, BirthDate, Relationship)
Note: {} represents multivalued attributes

4.6.1.4 Relationship Types to Database Schema

1. Manages
    Type: 1:1
    Participation: Employee as partial and department as total
    Attributes: start date

2. Works_for
    Type: 1:N
    Participation: Department as total and employee as total
    Attributes: NA

3. Controls
    Type: 1:N
    Participation: Project as total and department as partial
    Attributes: NA

4. Supervision
    Type: 1:N
    Participation: Employee as partial
    Attributes: NA

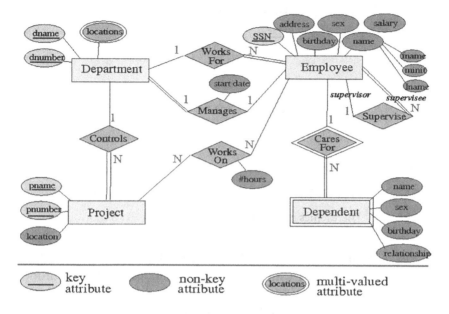

FIGURE 4.14 ER diagram for company.

5. Works_on
   Type: M:N
   Participation: Employee and projects as total
   Attributes: Hours

6. Dependents (weak entity type)
   Type: 1:N
   Participation: Employee as partial and dependent as total
   Attributes: NA

4.7 ENHANCED ER MODEL

Entity-relationship (ER) model having enhanced properties like inheritance, generalization, specialization, aggregation, etc. is called enhanced/extended ER model [8].

4.7.1 Hierarchies

One entity type might be a subtype of another – very **similar to subclasses** in object-oriented programming – which inherits the attributes and relationships of the first entity.

Air vehicle is a subtype of vehicle.

A relationship exists between an air vehicle entity and the corresponding vehicle entity, e.g., air vehicle airplane is related to **vehicle** airplane.

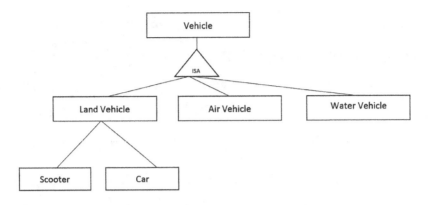

FIGURE 4.15 Hierarchies in the EER diagram.

This relationship is called **IsA**. Some texts will call this an IsA relationship, but **do not confuse** with the concept of relationship between entities.

- Airplane IsA vehicle, and a car IsA land vehicle.

- The two entities represented by IsA are always descriptions of the same real-world object.

- Typically used in databases to be implemented as object-oriented models.

- The upper entity type is the more abstract/general entity type (supertype) from which the lower entities inherit its attributes (Figure 4.15).

4.7.2 Properties of IsA Relationship Vehicle

Inheritance: All attributes of the supertype apply to the subtype, i.e., all the attributes of superclass will also be automatically present in subclasses, and apart from the inherited attributes, the subtypes can have their own attributes.

- e.g., registration number attribute of **vehicle** applies to **airplane**.

- **The subtype inherits all attributes of its supertype.**

- The key of the supertype is also the key of the subtype.

Transitivity – This property creates a hierarchy of IsA relationships.

- **Air vehicle** is a subtype of **vehicle**,
  car is a subtype of land vehicle,
  and therefore, **car** is also a subtype of **vehicle**.

Advantage: Used to make a more readable and succinct ER diagram. It better corresponds to object-oriented database or application approaches.

- Attributes common to multiple entity sets do not need to be repeated; instead, they can be grouped together as supertype attributes.

- The characteristics of (sibling) subtypes are likely to vary (and should be for this to be very useful).

4.7.3 Constraints in ER/EER Diagram

These associated constraints may apply to IsA hierarchies:

Covering Constraint: When the union of subtype entities equals the set of supertype entities, this property holds. At least one subtype is represented by an object.

All entities from water vehicle and entities from land vehicle are going to be the vehicle entity set.

Disjointness Constraint: When subtype entities are disjoint from one another, this holds true (i.e., the sets are mutually exclusive). An object may only be a part of another entity.

The entities from different entity sets are going to be different, i.e., if an entity is in one entity set, then the same will not be present in another entity set. It is going to be the unique entity.

It will be represented as overlapping if it is not disjoint.

4.7.4 Specialization Abstraction

Specialization: when a subset of an entity set has additional attributes or participates in specific, separate relationships.

Breaking down a class into subclasses is a process.

Example: Faculty contains fulltime and part-time

- Faculty has attributes **facid, lastName, firstName, rank**.

- Part-time also has **rateperhour**

- Fulltime has **Salary**

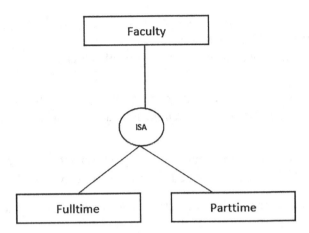

FIGURE 4.16   Specialization in the EER diagram.

It can be total or partial; if all the members of superclass are present in any of the subclasses, it is called total; otherwise, it will be called partial (Figure 4.16).

Specialization circle (IsA relationship) is depicted in the EER diagram.

Specialization may also be limited to a single subclass – no circle is needed, but the inheritance symbol must be shown.

The disjointedness constraint is most definitely being invoked by the subentities.

4.7.5 Generalization Abstraction

The classes having similar properties that can form a superclass is called generalization.

Ex. Air vehicle and water vehicle are both vehicle, Bottom-up process, as opposed to top-down process of specialization

EER diagram is similar for specialization

4.7.6 Union or Category

A subclass is connected to a group of superclasses. Each subclass instance belongs to one of the superclasses, not all of them. Superclasses, for example, form a union or group. A team, a department, or a club may be a sponsor. Owner is a subset of the union of person, bank, and company since each owner entity instance belongs to one of these superclasses.

In the EER diagram, each superclass connects with the union constraints, and subclasses also connect with the union constraints (Figure 4.17).

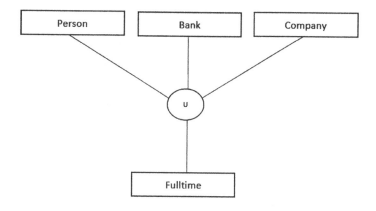

FIGURE 4.17   Union in the EER diagram.

4.8 REDUCTION OF ER DIAGRAM TO RELATIONAL MODEL [9]

1. Represent regular/strong entity

Build a new relational independent table for each strong entity collection that includes all attributes as columns. Only component attributes are included in the composite attribute.

2. Represent weak entity

Convert each weak entity set into a table with the discrimination attribute of the weak entity set as a primary key and the primary key of the strong entity set as a foreign key, and then declare the discriminator attribute and foreign key combination as a primary key.

3. Represent 1:1 Relationship

When two individuals S and T have a 1:1 relationship, choose one of the connections, such as S, and use the primary key of T as an international key in S. It is preferable to select complete participation of entities on S and provide descriptive attributes.

4. Represent 1:N Relationship

Identify the entity S on the N side of the relationship for a 1:N relationship. In S, add a foreign key. Relation T's primary key also includes 1:N attribute of S discipline attributes.

5. Represent N:N Relationship

Create a new relational table for each M:N relationship, including the primary key of the participating entities as well as descriptive

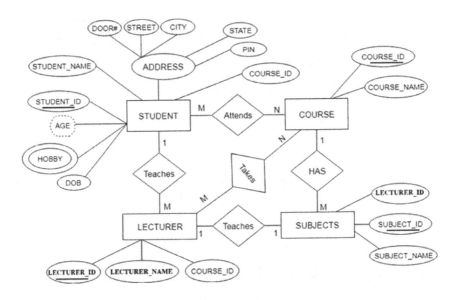

FIGURE 4.18   University ER diagram.

attributes. The table's primary key would be a combination of the primary keys of the participants.

6. Represent multivalued attribute

We will create a new table for each multivalued attribute, using the primary key of the main table as a foreign key and the multivalued attribute as the primary key (Figure 4.18).

Key points for converting an ER diagram to a table:

4.8.1 Regular Table

As per the above ER diagram, Student, Subject, Lecturer, and Course are going to be regular tables.

4.8.2 Attributes for the Table

All single-value attributes are going to be the columns of the tables. For example, in course table, course_id and course name are the columns.

4.8.3 Key Attribute (Primary Key)

The attributes underlined are known as key attributes and represented as primary key in the table, for example, student_id is represented as primary key in the student table.

4.8.4 Separate Table for Multivalued Attribute

An attribute having multiple values is known as a multivalued attribute, and it is going to represent as a separate table including the primary key of the representing entity set and multivalued attribute. For example, hobby is a multivalued attribute in a student table.

4.8.5 Derived Attributes

It's an attribute not considered in the table as it can be calculated with the help of other attributes; for example, age is the derived attribute in the student table that can be calculated by current date and date of birth.

Based on the above rule, the following relations are going to be created and mapped between the different relations (Figure 4.19).

4.8.6 Mapping of Relationships in the Tables

As mentioned above, we will have mapping into four categories: 1:1, 1:N, N:1, and M:N types of relationships. In case of 1:1, 1:N, and N:1 relationship types, only the existing tables will be updated, but in the case of M:N relationships, a new table will be created by the name of relationships having the primary keys of both the participating tables and its own attribute.

As per the above ER diagram, two new tables will be created for M:N relationship types: attends and takes.

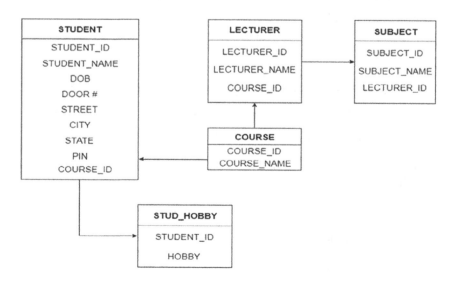

FIGURE 4.19   Reduction in tables.

Attends (Student_Id, Course_ID)

Takes (Lecturer_ID, Course_ID)

Furthermore, as per the relationships, the tables will be updated.

1:1 relationship mapping: Lecturer and subjects have 1:1 mapping in the above ER diagram, so we can choose any one of the entity sets as S and the other as T. Let lecturer be S and subject be T; then the relation will become

Lecturer (Lecturer_Id, Lecturer_name, Course_Id, Subject_Id)

Subject (Subject_Id, Subject_name)

Note: In 1:1 relationship, if the participation is total, then we will make the entity set that totally participated S.

1:N & N:1 Relationship Mapping- In this the entity set participating by N, make as S. In the above ER- Diagram two 1:N or N:1 relationships.

Let's take student and Lecturer where student participates by 1 in the teaches relationship while lecturer participates by N in the teaches relationships so primary key of student will be act as foreign key in the lecturer relation, then the relations will be.

Student (Student_Id, Student_name, DOB, Door#, street, city, state, pin, course_Id)

Lecturer (Lecturer_Id, Lecturer_name, Course_Id, Student_Id, Subject_Id)

Another 1:N relationship is course and subject where course will become T and subject will become S because subject participates an N in the relationship, so the relations will be as follows:

Course (course_Id, Course_name)

Subject (Subject_id, Subject_name, course_id)

Now, the final relations are as follows:

a. Student (Student_Id, Student_name, DOB, Door#, street, city, state, pin, course_Id)

b. Course (course_Id, Course_name)

c. Lecturer (Lecturer_Id, Lecturer_name, Course_Id, Student_Id, Subject_Id)

d. Subject (Subject_id, Subject_name, course_id)

e. Attends (Student_Id, Course_ID)

f. Takes (Lecturer_ID, Course_ID)

g. Student hobby (Student_Id, hobby)

4.8.7 Tables

Create table student
  (
  Student_Id varchar(10),
  Student_name varchar(20),
  DOB date,
  Door# integer,
  Street varchar(10),
  City varchar(20),
  State varchar(20),
  Pin integer,
  Course_id varchar(20),
  Primary Key (student_Id)
  );
  Create table course
  (
  Course_Id varchar(20),
  Course_name varchar (20),
  Primary Key (course_Id)
  );
  Create table subject
  (
  Subject_Id varchar(10),
  Subject_name varchar (20),
  Course_id varchar(20),
  Primary Key (Subject_Id),
  Foreign key (course_Id) references course
  );
  Create table lecturer
  (
  Lecturer_Id varchar(10),
  Lecturer_name varchar(20),
  Course_id varchar(10),
  Subject_Id varchar(10),
  Student_Id varchar(10),
  Primary Key(Lecturer_Id),
  Foreign key(subject_Id) references subject,
  Foreign key(student_Id) references student
)

Create table attends

(

Student_Id varchar(10),

Course_Id varchar (10),

Primary Key (Student_Id, Course_Id),

Foreign key(student_Id) references student,

Foreign key(course_Id) references course

);

Create table takes

(

Lecturer_Id varchar(10),

Course_Id varchar (10),

Primary Key (Lecturer_Id, Course_Id),

Foreign key(Lecturer_Id) references Lecturer,

Foreign key(course_Id) references course

);

Create table studenthobby

(

student_Id varchar(10),

Hobby varchar (10),

Primary Key (Student_Id, Hobby),

Foreign key(student_Id) references student,

);

4.9 SUMMARY

In this chapter, we focused on the ER model and enhanced ER model with all the characteristics of these models like entity sets, attributes, and type of relationships, e.g., one-to-one, one-to-many, many-to-one, and many-to-many. Various constraints like participation, disjoint, overlapping, etc. make the ER/EER diagram more effective. We have also discussed how to manage the many-to-many relationship and its implementation in the database.

We also showed how a conceptual schema design in the ER model can be mapped to a relational database schema. An algorithm for ER-to-relational mapping was given and illustrated by examples from the COMPANY database. We summarized the correspondences between the ER and relational model constructs and constraints. Similar algorithms are incorporated into graphical database design tools to create a relational schema from a conceptual schema design automatically.

4.10 REVIEW QUESTIONS

1. Imagine that you have been assigned to a team that will be developing an inventory tracking system. As part of the project startup, your manager has asked each team leader to bring a basic work plan to the next meeting. At that meeting, these work plans will be analyzed to determine the overall project timeframe, costs, personnel requirements, and software requirements. For now, as the team leader for the data design team, you have been asked to bring a work plan that identifies the phases of data design and includes the following information for each phase:

   a. A description of the data design phase,

   b. The inputs of the phase,

   c. The outputs of the phase,

   d. A key issue addressed in the phase,

   e. A challenge that you can anticipate would occur in the phase.

   Prepare the response you will bring to the meeting.

2. UPS prides itself on having up-to-date information on the processing and current location of each shipped item. To do this, UPS relies on a company-wide information system. Shipped items are the heart of the UPS product tracking information system. Shipped items can be characterized by item number (unique), weight, dimensions, insurance amount, destination, and final delivery date. Shipped items are received into the UPS system at a single retail center. Retail centers are characterized by their type, unique ID, and address. Shipped items make their way to their destination via one or more standard UPS transportation events (i.e., flights, truck deliveries). These transportation events are characterized by a unique schedule number, a type (e.g., flight, truck), and a delivery route.

   Create an ER diagram that captures this information about the UPS system. Be certain to indicate identifiers and cardinality constraints.

3. Production tracking is important in many manufacturing environments (e.g., the pharmaceuticals industry, children's toys). The following ER diagram captures important information in the tracking

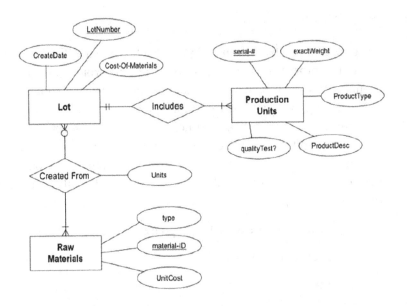

FIGURE 4.20   ER diagram for manufacturing site.

of production. Specifically, the ER diagram captures relationships between production lots (or batches), individual production units, and raw materials. Convert the ER diagram into a relational database schema. Be certain to indicate primary keys and referential integrity constraints (Figure 4.20).

4. Assume we have the following application that models soccer teams, the games they play, and the players in each team. In the design, we want to capture the following:

- We have a set of teams, and each team has an ID (unique identifier), name, main stadium, and a city to which this team belongs.

- Each team has many players, and each player belongs to one team. Each player has a number (unique identifier), name, DoB, start year, and shirt number that he uses.

- Teams play matches; in each match, there is a host team and a guest team. The match takes place in the stadium of the host team.

- For each match, we need to keep track of the following: The date on which the game is played, the final result of the match, and the players participated in the match. For each player, how many goals he scored, whether or not he took yellow card, and whether or not he took red card. During the match, one player may substitute another player. We want to capture this substitution and the time at which it took place. Each match has exactly three referees. For each referee, we have an ID (unique identifier), name, DoB, and years of experience. One referee is the main referee, and the other two are assistant referees. Design an ER diagram to capture the above requirements. State any assumptions you have that affects your design (use the back of the page if needed). Make sure cardinalities and primary keys are clear.

5. What are the most common errors you can potentially face in data modeling?

6. In the context of data modeling, what is the importance of metadata?

7. Have you ever come across the scenario of recursive relationships? If yes, how did you handle it?

8. What is the number of child tables that can be created out from a single parent table?

9. If a unique constraint is applied to a column, then will it throw an error if you try to insert two nulls into it?

10. How is the entity, entity type, and entity set different from each other in a DBMS?

REFERENCES

1. Bill Smith, "Systems Building with Oracle- The Theory and Practice of Database Design" https://doi.org/10.1007/978-0-230-00094-0.
2. Difference between Strong and Weak Entity (12 November 2020), https://www.geeksforgeeks.org/difference-between-strong-and-weak-entity/.
3. Types of Relationships (11 March 2021), University of Portsmouth.
4. Semantic Data Modeling (10 December 2020), http://docplayer.net/28613239-Part-2-semantic-data-modeling.html.
5. Many to Many Relationships (13 October 2020), https://www.baeldung.com/jpa-many-to-many.

6. Create Many to Many Relationships (22 April 2021), https://success.outsystems.com/Documentation/11/Developing_an_Application/Use_Data/Data_Modeling/Entity_Relationships/Create_a_Many-to-Many_Relationship.

7. MicroStrategy Advanced Reporting Guide (12 June 2021), https://manualzz.com/doc/48787632/microstrategy-advanced-reporting-guide.

8. Enhanced Entity-Relationship Model (17 April 2021), http://jcsites.juniata.edu/faculty/Rhodes/dbms/eermodel.htm.

9. Conversion of ER Diagram to Relational Model (17 March 2021), https://www.includehelp.com/dbms/conversion-of-er-diagram-to-relational-model.aspx.

CHAPTER 5

Normalization

5.1 INTRODUCTION TO NORMALIZATION – A BOTTOM-UP APPROACH

Normalization is a process of designing a database schema in a way to reduce redundancy or duplication of record and eliminate various anomalies from a database like insert anomaly, update anomaly, and delete anomaly. The normalization process takes a relation schema through a sequence of tests to formally declare whether it satisfies the requirements of a certain normal form [1,2]. This process, which involves evaluation of each relation against the conditions for normal forms, is considered as relational design by analysis.

5.2 NEED FOR NORMALIZATION

Normalization is an important process in designing a good database and eliminating the flaws of a bad database design. A badly designed database has issues in adding and deleting records from a table and makes the table data in an inconstant state. Normalization is a process of decomposition of a large relation into two or more relations to remove the abovementioned anomalies. The decomposition is performed on the basis of some predefined rules. The division into multiple relations should be such that there are common keys in two or more decomposed relations so that using that common key or attribute allows retrieval of the complete record. In short, the decomposition should be a lossless division, and the join should be a lossless join.

DOI: 10.1201/9780429282843-5

The major advantages of normalization are given below:

1. It reduces the complexity of a big relation.

2. It helps to reduce redundancy of record in a relation.

3. It helps to eliminate various anomalies in a database.

4. It also helps to maintain atomicity in a relation.

5. Various normal forms of normalization are used to address different kinds of issues of a relation.

5.3 TYPES OF DEPENDENCIES

Function dependency (FD) represents the relationship between two or more attributes in a given relation. It may represent the relationship between key attribute and nonkey attribute or between two nonkey attributes. The notation used for FD between two attributes X, Y of a relation is given below

$X \rightarrow Y$

Here, the left-side attribute, i.e., X in this case, is called determinant, and the right-side attribute, i.e., Y, is called dependent.

There are two types of functional dependencies as shown in the following diagram (Figure 5.1).

5.3.1 Trivial FD

A FD $X \rightarrow Y$ will be called trivial FD if Y is a subset of X. A self-based FD, e.g., $X \rightarrow X$ or $Y \rightarrow Y$, is also an example of trivial FD [3–5].

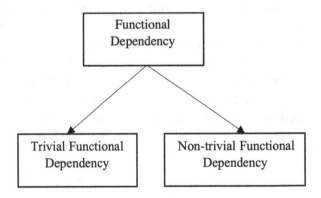

FIGURE 5.1   Types of FD.

Consider the following relation Employee

Employee	
EID	EName

In this relation,

{EID, EName} → EID is a trivial FD as EID is a subset of {EID, EName}.
Also, EID → EID and EName → EName are trivial dependencies.

5.3.2 Nontrivial FD

A FD X → Y will be called nontrivial FD if Y is not a subset of X. If X and Y
are such a set of attributes of a dependency where X intersection Y is null,
then X → Y is called complete nontrivial FD.

Consider the following relation Employee

Employee		
EID	EName	DOB

In this relation,

EID → EName is a nontrivial FD.
Also, EID → DOB is also a nontrivial FD.

5.3.3 Armstrong's Axioms or Inference Rule of Functional Dependencies

There are six inference rules or Armstrong's axioms of FD. Using these
rules, more FDs can be identified from a given initial set of dependency
[6,7].

1. **Reflexivity rule:** If α is a set of attributes and $\beta \subseteq \alpha$ then $\alpha \to \beta$ holds.

2. **Augmentation rule:** If $\alpha \to \beta$ holds, and γ is a set of attributes, then $\gamma\alpha \to \gamma\beta$ holds.

3. **Transitivity rule:** If $\alpha \to \beta$ holds, and $\beta \to \gamma$ holds, then $\alpha \to \gamma$ holds.

4. **Union rule:** If $\alpha \to \beta$ holds, and $\alpha \to \gamma$ holds, then $\alpha \to \beta\gamma$ holds.

5. **Decomposition rule:** If $\alpha \to \beta\gamma$ holds, then $\alpha \to \beta$ holds, and $\alpha \to \gamma$ holds.

6. **Pseudotransitivity rule:** If $\alpha \rightarrow \gamma$ holds, and $\gamma\beta \rightarrow \delta$ holds, then $\alpha\gamma \rightarrow \delta$ holds.

5.4 FIRST NORMAL FORM

A relation will be called in first normal form (1NF) if it holds the following properties

1. Each cell should contain an atomic value.

2. Any attribute should not have multiple values.

3. A relation should not have a multivalued attribute, composite attribute, and their combination.

Example:
The following relation named EMPLOYEE is not in 1NF because it has multivalued attribute.

EMPLOYEE table

EID	ENAME	MOBILE_NO	CITY
1001	Amit	9410211023, 7890911034	Delhi
1002	Karan	8755362134	Mumbai
1003	John	7865891452, 9877009452	Dehradun

The representation of the above table into 1NF is shown below where separate rows have been added for each mobile number to eliminate maintaining atomic value in each cell.

EID	ENAME	MOBILE_NO	CITY
1001	Amit	9410211023	Delhi
1001	Amit	7890911034	Delhi
1002	Karan	8574783832	Mumbai
1003	John	7865891452	Dehradun
1003	John	9877009452	Dehradun

5.5 SECOND NORMAL FORM

A relation will be called in second normal form (2NF) if it holds the following properties:

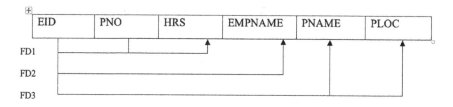

FIGURE 5.2   EMP_Proj relation.

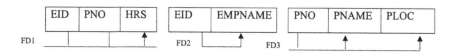

FIGURE 5.3   Decomposition of EMP-Proj relation.

1. It should be in 1NF.

2. All nonprime attributes should be fully functional dependent on a prime attribute.

Example:

Consider the following relation EMP_PROJ. This relation is not in 2NF. FD2 and FD3 violate the rule for 2NF. EMPNAME, PNAME, and PLOC are not fully dependent on prime attribute (EID, PNO). This violates the 2NF condition (Figure 5.2).

The decomposition of the above relation is shown below to fulfill the conditions of 2NF. The FDs FD1, FD2, and FD3 now fulfill the second condition of 2NF as all nonprime attributes are fully dependent on prime attributes. Now, a non-2NF relation EMPLOYEE is decomposed into three relations EMP1, EMP2, and EMP3, which follow 2NF norms and are given below (Figure 5.3).

5.6   THIRD NORMAL FORM

A relation will be called in third normal form (3NF) if it holds the following properties

1. It should be in 2NF.

2. There should not be any transitive dependency.

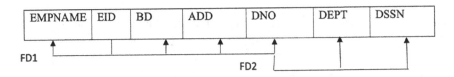

FIGURE 5.4   EMP-Dept relation.

This normal form is used to reduce data redundancy and provide data integrity.

Example:

The relation given in the following example named EMP_DEPT is in 2NF but not in 3NF as DSSN is transitive-dependent on EID via DNO. So, this relation contains transitive dependency, which violates the condition of 3NF. To make this relation into 3NF, we need to decompose this relation into two relations as given below. So, we have divided the relation EMP_DEPT into two relations ED1 and ED2, which does not contain any transitive dependency. Hence, these two relations are now in 3NF (Figure 5.4).

5.7 BOYCE-CODD NORMAL FORM

Boyce-Codd normal form (BCNF) is a more restricted form of 3NF. A relation will be in BCNF if it holds the following properties:

1. The relation should be in 3NF.

2. A relation is in BCNF if every dependency contains determinant attributes as the candidate key of the table.

Example:

Let us consider the following EMPLOYEE table where the employee works in different departments.

EMPLOYEE table

EID	CITY	DNAME	D_TYPE	DNO
101	Delhi	Accounting	D10	201
101	Delhi	Development	D10	301
102	Mumbai	Admin	D20	202
102	Mumbai	Testing	D20	304

The FD in this relation is given below:

EID → CITY

DNAME → {D_TYPE, DNO}

Candidate key: {EID, DNAME}

The given EMPLOYEE table in not in BCNF as EID and DNAME are not keys in individual. To convert this table into BCNF, we have to decompose it into three tables.

E_CITY table

EID	CITY
101	Delhi
102	Mumbai

E_DEPT table

DNAME	D_TYPE	DNO
Accounting	D10	201
Development	D10	301
Admin	D20	202
Testing	D20	304

E_DEPT_MAPPING table

EID	DNO
101	201
101	301
102	202
102	304

FDs of the tables are as follows:

EID → CITY

DNAME → {D_TYPE, DNO}

Candidate keys of the tables are as follows:

For E_CITY table: EID

For E_DEPT table: DNAME

For E_DEPT_MAPPING table: {EID, DNAME }

5.8 MULTI-VALUED DEPENDENCY

Multivalued dependency occurs when there are two attributes that are completely independent from each other but dependent on a third attribute. For multivalued dependency, at least three attributes are needed in a relation. When one or more rows in a table implies one or more other rows in the same table, then multivalued dependency occurs. It violates the rule of 4NF [8,9].

It is represented by ->->. If a table contains three columns A, B, and C, then in case of multivalued dependency,

A->-> B

A->->C

In this representation, multivalued dependency exists only if B and C are independent variables.

An example of multivalued dependency that violates 4NF is given below.

Employee

Ename	Project	Hobbies
John	AWS	Cricket
John	AWS	Reading
Alice	NodeJS	Dancing
Alice	NodeJS	Singing
Alice	NodeJS	Playing

In the above employee table, we can find that John and Alice have more than one hobby. This contains multivalued dependency because project is independent of hobbies. But dependent on the employee.

Hence, the multivalued dependencies are as follows:

Ename->-> Project

Ename->-> Hobbies

Thus, the above relation violates the 4NF rule. To make this single relation into 4NF, we have to divide it into two relations in the following way:

Employee_Project

Ename	Project
John	AWS
John	AWS
Alice	NodeJS
Alice	NodeJS
Alice	NodeJS

Employee_Hobbies	
Ename	**Hobbies**
John	Cricket
John	Reading
Alice	Dancing
Alice	Singing
Alice	Playing

After breaking the main table into two tables, we have two normal dependencies as follows.

In Employee_Project relation, we have the following FD.

Ename ->Project

In Employee_Hobbies relation, we have the following FD.

Ename->Hobbies

5.9 JOIN DEPENDENCY

1. Join dependency (JD) is a concept in which if we join two decomposed relations R1 and R2 of a nonnormalized relation R, then the result of the join should be all attributes of R.

2. R1 and R2 are the decompositions R1(A, B, C) and R2(C, D) of a given relation R (A, B, C, D).

3. If the join of R1 and R2 over C is equal to relation R, then we can say that a JD exists.

4. Alternatively, R1 and R2 are lossless decompositions of R.

5. A JD ⋈ {R1, R2,..., Rn} is said to hold over a relation R if R1, R2,....., Rn is a lossless-join decomposition.

6. The *(A, B, C, D), (C, D) will be a JD of R if the join of join's attribute is equal to the relation R.

7. Here, *(R1, R2, R3) is used to indicate that relation R1, R2, R3 and so on are a JD of R.

5.10 LOSSLESS AND LOSSY DECOMPOSITIONS

As we have discussed in normalization, to normalize a given relation, we need to decompose it into two or more relations. The decomposition process can be done in two manners.

1. Lossless decomposition

2. Lossy decomposition

If we decompose a relation R into multiple relations R1, R2, R3......Rn and if the following conditions hold [10]:

R1 ⋈ R2 ⋈ R3.... ⋈ Rn = R

then the performed decomposition is lossless decomposition. If the above condition is not satisfied, then the decomposition is lossy decomposition.

5.11 NORMALIZING TABLES AND UNSOLVED EXAMPLES WITH CASE STUDIES

1. Consider a relation R with five attributes A, B, C, D, and E. You are given the following dependencies,

   $A \rightarrow B, BC \rightarrow E, ED \rightarrow A$.

   a. List all keys of R

   b. Is R in 3NF?

2. A database is designed as a single table consisting of the following columns. Use normalization to improve design.

   Table (Stu_no, S_Name, S_Addr, Course_name, Teacher_Name, Teacher_room_no, Marks_obt).

5.12 SUMMARY

Normalization is a process of decomposition of a big relation into small relations to eliminate various insert, update, and delete anomalies. FD is an integrity constraint that generalizes the concept of a key. Many additional functional dependencies can be identified from a given set of initial FDs using the FD inference rule. To achieve the nonredundancy and data integrity feature in RDBMS, normalization provides 1NF, 2NF, 3NF, BCNF, and 4NF normal forms to fine-tune the schema of a given database. The given nonnormalized schema should be decomposed in such way that it should have lossless dependency. It means that the complete list of attributes should be regenerated once joining all decomposed relations, and data should not be lost.

5.13 REVIEW QUESTIONS

1. Explain FD with the help of an example.

2. List and discuss Armstrong's six axioms related to FD?

3. Describe the need of normalization. How is it useful for data integrity?

4. Write a short note on the following with an example.

   a. First normal Form (1NF)

   b. Second normal Form (2NF)

   c. Third normal Form (3NF)

5. Is BCNF stronger than 3NF? Explain with an example.

REFERENCES

1. A. Aboulnaga and S. Chaudhuri, "Self-Tuning histograms: Building histograms without looking at data", Proceedings of the ACM International Conference on Management of Data, 1999.
2. C. Konig, A. Kraiss, M. Sinnewell, and G. Weikum, "Towards Self- Tuning Memory Management for Data Servers", *Bulletin of the Technical Committee on Data Engineering, IEEE Computer Society*, vol. 22, No. 1, pp. 3–11, 1999.
3. H. K. Sharma, S. Kumar, S. Dubey, and P. Gupta, "Auto-Selection and Management of Dynamic SGA Parameters in RDBMS", International Conference on Computing for Sustainable Global Development, INDIACom, pp. 1763–1768, 2015.
4. H. K. Sharma and M. S. C. Nelson, "Performance enhancement using SQL statement tuning approach", *Database Systems Journal*, vol. 8, no. 1, pp. 12–21, 2017.
5. A. Shastri, R. Biswas, and S. K. Singh, "SGA Dynamic Parameters: The Core Components of Automated Database Tuning", *Database Systems Journal*, vol. 5, no. 2, pp. 13–21, 2014.
6. M. S. C. Nelson, "Explain Plan and SQL Trace the Two Approaches for RDBMS Tuning", *Database Systems Journal*, vol. 8, no. 1, pp. 31–39, 2017.
7. H. K. Sharma and S. K. Singh, "Tuning I/O Subsystem: A Key Component in RDBMS Performance Tuning", *Database Systems Journal*, vol. 7, no. 1, pp. 3–11, 2016.
8. H. K. Sharma, A. Shastri, and R. Biswas, "An Algorithmic Approach for Auto-Selection of Resources to Self-Tune the Database", *IJRIT International Journal of Research in Information Technology*, vol. 1, no. 9, pp. 288–289, 2013.

9. H. K. Sharma, A. Shastri, and R. Biswas, "ARH_Db_Tuner The GUI tool to Monitor and Diagnose the SGA Parameters Automatically", *Database Systems Journal*, vol. 4, no. 1, 2013.

10. R. Biswas, "A Framework for Automated Database Tuning Using Dynamic SGA Parameters and Basic Operating System Utilities", *Database System Journal Romania*, 2013.

CHAPTER 6

Managing Data Using Structured Query Language

6.1 INTRODUCTION TO STRUCTURED QUERY LANGUAGE

Structured query language (SQL) is a high-level computer language used by relational database management systems (RDBMSs) for database interaction. It is used to define, create, and manage the databases [1, 2]. RDBMSs are getting popularity because of their ease of access using this high-level programming language. SQL is further divided into various types based on its functionality with databases.

6.1.1 Advantages of SQL

It is not a simple procedural programming language where the logic will be interpreted in a step-by-step manner. As any procedural programming language, SQL also follows a standard syntax. ANSI and ISO are the standardization body, which provide and maintain the standard syntax for all RDBMS providers [3–5]. All RDBMSs need to follow at least 80% syntax of ANSI SQL standard. The major advantages of SQL are given below:

1. SQL has well-defined standards provided by standard organizations like ANSI.

DOI: 10.1201/9780429282843-6

2. SQL is a portable language; it can be executed on small- and large-scale computing devices.

3. It is easy to integrate with multiple platforms, and data can be transferred from one platform to another platform.

4. SQL can also be used to define data structure, control access to the data, and delete, insert, and modify the occurrence of the data.

5. SQL has its division of command sets as per its functionalities. Data definition language (DDL), data manipulation language (DML) data query language (DQL), data control language (DCL), and transaction control language (TCL) are such subdivisions.

6. PL/SQL is another additional module in SQL, which makes it possible to write business login on a database.

These are some major advantages of SQL. It is simple to read and write. The syntax and semantic used in writing SQL are simple to learn, and after a basic knowledge of this syntax, a simple learner can easily write these queries.

6.1.2 Types of SQL Commands

SQL statements are used to create a table, insert data into a table, update the data in the existing table, delete the data from the table, and take control on various entities of DBMS. An SQL command is a set of instruction-based keywords to be executed on a DBMS to find the required information. SQL commands can be classified into several categories. The various types of SQL commands are given below.

- DDL

- DML

- DQL

- DCL

- TCL

6.2 DATA DEFINITION COMMANDS

These commands are used for defining and manipulating the structure of a database and tables. These commands are also used to create and manipulate other database objects as well such as user, views, and triggers. Here are the list of commands used for DDL [6].

CREATE: Create command is used to create any kind of object in a database. It is used to create table, user, view, etc.

The syntax to create a table in a DBMS is given below:

```
CREATE TABLE
<TABLE_NAME>
(<COLUMN_NAME> <DATATYPES[,....]>);
```

Example:

```
CREATE TABLE EMPLOYEE
(
    EMPNO NUMBER(5),
    ENAME CHAR(30),
    AGE NUMBER(3),
);
```

This command will create a structure of a table Employee.

Employee		
Empno	Ename	Age

ALTER: Alter command is used to modify the existing object in a database including table, user, and views.

The syntax to alter a table in a DBMS is given below:

```
ALTER TABLE
<TABLE_NAME>
ADD
<COLUMN_NAME>
COLUMN-DEFINITION;
```

Example:

```
ALTER TABLE
EMPLOYEE
ADD
(SAL NUMBER(10));
```

This command will add a new attribute in the existing table Employee.

Employee			
Empno	Ename	Age	Sal

DROP: Drop command is used to drop an existing object of a database including table, user, and views.

Syntax

DROP TABLE
<TABLE NAME>;

Example

DROP TABLE
EMPLOYEE;

TRUNCATE: Truncate command is used to delete the data of the entire table, but contains the schema of the table.

Syntax:

TRUNCATE TABLE
<TABLE NAME>;

Example:

TRUNCATE TABLE
EMPLOYEE;

6.3 DML

DML is used for manipulation of records in a table. It is used for inserting, updating, and deleting the records in a table or from a table. The commands falling in this category are not auto-committed. It means that the records changed with these commands can be rolled back if not committed explicitly [7, 8].

INSERT Command:

The INSERT statement is a SQL query. It is used to insert data into the row of a table.

Syntax:

INSERT
INTO
<TABLE_NAME> (<col1>, <col2>.... col N)
VALUES (<value1>, <value2>,.... <valueN>);

Or

INSERT
INTO
<TABLE_NAME>
VALUES (<value1>, <value2>,.... <valueN>);

For example:
INSERT
INTO
EMPLOYEE (Empno, Ename, Age)
VALUES (101, "Amit", 28);

This command will insert a tuple or row in the table created in the previous DDL command.

Employee		
Empno	Ename	Age
101	Amit	28

UPDATE Command:

This DML command is used to update the old value with the new value of one or more attributes of a table based on a condition. If the condition is not given with update command, then all values of the mentioned columns will be updated with the new value [9, 10].

Syntax:

UPDATE
<TABLE_NAME>
SET [col1= value1,...colN=valueN]
[WHERE CONDITION];

Or

UPDATE
<TABLE_NAME>
SET [col1= value1,...colN = valueN]

For example:
Suppose we have the following Employee table:

Employee		
Empno	Ename	Age
101	Amit	28
102	Kabir	30
103	Monika	25
104	Kavita	35

On executing the following update command

UPDATE
EMPLOYEE
SET AGE=38
WHERE ID=101

We will get the following updated Employee table (updated value is highlighted):

Employee		
Empno	Ename	Age
101	Amit	38
102	Kabir	30
103	Monika	25
104	Kavita	35

If we execute update command without where clause, then it will update all rows of that column with the same value.

Example:

UPDATE
EMPLOYEE
SET AGE=38

We will get the following updated Employee table (updated value is highlighted):

Employee		
Empno	Ename	Age
101	Amit	38
102	Kabir	38
103	Monika	38
104	Kavita	38

DELETE Command:

This DML command is used to delete some specific records or all records from a table. This command will delete all records from a table where the specified condition will be matched. If a condition is not specified with DELETE command, then all records will be deleted from a table [11, 12].

Syntax:
DELETE
FROM
<TABLE_NAME>
[WHERE condition];

For example:

DELETE
FROM
EMPLOYEE
WHERE EMPNO=102;

After executing the above DELETE command, we will get a record deleted from the Employee table whose Empno is 102

Employee		
Empno	Ename	Age
101	Amit	38
103	Monika	25
104	Kavita	35

6.4 DATA CONTROL LANGUAGE

DCL commands are used to give and take access privileges to a user or from a user. These commands can be used to give or take privileges at various levels of a database object. There are many privileges and roles available in an RDBMS, which can be Grant and Revoke.

There are the following two commands used in DCL.

6.4.1 GRANT Command

It is used to give access privileges to users of a database. Using Grant command, accessing privileges are given to the specific users.

Syntax:

GRANT
<List of Privileges>
ON
<TABLE_NAME>
TO
<USER_NAME>;

Example
GRANT
SELECT, UPDATE
ON
EMPLOYEE
TO
USER1

On execution of this command, the USER1 will get the permissions of selection and updation on the table EMPLOYEE.

6.4.2 REVOKE Command

It is used to take back permissions from the user.

Syntax:

REVOKE
<List of Privileges>
ON

<TABLE_NAME>
FROM
<USER_NAME>;

Example
REVOKE
SELECT, UPDATE
ON
EMPLOYEE
FROM
USER1

On execution of this command, permissions of selection and updation on the table EMPLOYEE will be revoked from USER1.

6.5 TRANSACTION CONTROL LANGUAGE (TCL)

TCL is used to control DML command's output. INSERT, UPDATE, and DELETE commands do not perform permanent changes on a database. These changes can be rolled back or saved permanently to the last safe point using these commands. These commands can be executed after any DML command [13].

Here are some commands that come under TCL:

6.5.1 COMMIT Command

Commit command is used to save all changes done by DML commands on a database. The data cannot be rolled back once COMMIT command is executed.

Syntax:
COMMIT;

Example:
DELETE
FROM
EMPLOYEE
WHERE Empno = 101;

COMMIT;

6.5.2 ROLLBACK Command

Rollback command is used to UNDO the changes done after DML commands. If the changes done by Insert, Update, and Delete commands on a table data are not acceptable, then using rollback, we can undo the data up to a stable state [9].

Syntax:
ROLLBACK;

Example:
DELETE
FROM
EMPLOYEE
WHERE
Empno = 101;

ROLLBACK;

SAVEPOINT Command: SAVEPOINT command is used to create a certain point up to which a rollback can be performed. Using savepoint, we can create a point that specifies the stable state of a database.

Syntax:

SAVEPOINT
<SAVEPOINT_NAME>;

6.6 DATA QUERY LANGUAGE (DQL)

DQL is a type of SQL command used to retrieve the record from a database table. This category of command is used to view required records from a database table using certain clauses defined in DQL command [12].

SELECT Command:
This is the same as the projection operation of relational algebra. It is used to select the attribute based on the condition described by WHERE clause.

Syntax:
SELECT
EXPRESSIONS

FROM
TABLES
WHERE CONDITIONS;

For example:

SELECT
emp_name
FROM
employee
WHERE Empno > 101;

6.7 AGGREGATE FUNCTIONS

Aggregate functions are used with Select command. These are applied on a set of values and returns a single value. These are also used with HAVING and GROUP BY clause. These are also known as single scaler functions.

Aggregate functions are used to perform calculation on a set of values and returns a single vale. These are also known as single scalar value function. These functions are used with GROUP BY and Having clause.

Majorly used aggregate functions are given below:

- **COUNT** – It is used to count the number of rows in a table or view.

- **SUM** – It is used to find the sum of all values of a column. It is applied on an integer-valued column.

- **AVG** – It is used to calculate the average of all values specified in select command.

- **MIN** – It is used to find the minimum value from a specified column of a table or view.

- **MAX** – It is used to find the maximum value from a specified column of a table or view.

COUNT Function: This function is used for counting the number of rows in a table or view. It can be applied on integer and character data type. COUNT(*) will count all rows and included duplicate and NULL values [12,13].

Syntax:
COUNT(*)
Or
COUNT([ALL|DISTINCT] expression)

We will take again the same table Employee with some additional rows to illustrate the use of these functions.

Employee				
Empno	Ename	Age	Sal	Dept
101	Amit	38	2000	10
102	Kabir	30	4500	20
103	Monika	25	3000	10
104	Kavita	35	3000	30
105	Karan	34	5000	30

Example:
SELECT
COUNT(*)
FROM EMPLOYEE;

Output:
5

Example: COUNT with WHERE
SELECT
COUNT(*)
FROM EMPLOYEE
WHERE SAL>=4000;

Output:
2

SELECT
COUNT(DISTINCT DEPT)
FROM EMPLOYEE;

Output:
3

```
SELECT DEPT, COUNT(*)
FROM EMPLOYEE
GROUP BY DEPT;
```

Output:
DEPT COUNT(*)
10 2
20 1
30 2

```
SELECT
DEPT, COUNT(*)
FROM EMPLOYEE
GROUP BY DEPT HAVING COUNT(*)=2;
```

Output:
DEPT COUNT(*)
10 2
30 2

SUM Function: This function is used for integer column only. It is used to find the sum of values for a given attribute.

Syntax
SUM()

Or

SUM([ALL|DISTINCT] expression)

Example:
```
SELECT
SUM(SAL)
FROM EMPLOYEE;
```

Output:
17,500

```
SELECT
SUM(SAL)
```

FROM EMPLOYEE
WHERE DEPT=10;

Output:
5000
SELECT
DEPT, SUM(SAL)
FROM EMPLOYEE
GROUP BY DEPT;

Output:
DEPT SUM(SAL)
10   5000
20   4500
30   8000

Example: SUM() with HAVING
SELECT DEPT, SUM(SAL)
FROM EMPLOYEE
GROUP BY DEPT
HAVING SUM(SAL)>6000;

Output:
DEPT SUM(SAL)
30 8000

AVG Function: This function is applied on an integer-valued column. It will return the average of the values present in a column. It will give an average of all not-null values.

Syntax
AVG()
or
AVG([ALL|DISTINCT] expression)

Example:
SELECT
AVG(SAL)
FROM EMPLOYEE;

Output:
3500

MAX Function: This aggregate function is applied on the integer column. It is used to find the maximum value from a given column of values.

Syntax
MAX()
or
MAX([ALL|DISTINCT] expression)

Example:
SELECT
MAX(SAL)
FROM EMPLOYEE;

Output:
5000

MIN Function: This aggregate function is applied on the integer column. It is used to find the minimum value from a given column of values.

Syntax
MIN()
or
MIN ([ALL|DISTINCT] expression)

Example:
SELECT
MIN(SAL)
FROM EMPLOYEE;

Output:
2000

6.8 DATE AND TIME FUNCTIONS

In SQL, there are many situations where we have to change the format of date as per the requirement of the user. SQL provides several data and time functions which help a query write to achieve this goal [7].

Some majorly used date and time functions with their explanation are given below.

CURDATE(): This function will return the current date of the system.
SELECT
CURDATE()
FROM DUAL;

Output:
14-MAY-2021

DATEDIFF(): This function will return the difference of two dates in no. of days.

SELECT
DATEDIFF('20-MAY-2021', '10-MAY-2021')
FROM DUAL;

Output:
10

ADDDATE(): This function will return the new date after adding the no. of days given as the second argument of function.

SELECT
ADDDATE('20-MAY-2021', 5)
FROM DUAL;

Output:
25-MAY-2021

DAYNAME(): This function will return the weekday name of a given date.

SELECT
DAYNAME('14-MAY-2021')
FROM DUAL;

Output:
Friday

DAYOFWEEK(): This function will return the index of the day in a week. (1= Sunday, 7=Saturday)

SELECT
DAYOFWEEK('14-MAY-2021')
FROM DUAL;

Output:
6

DAYOFYEAR(): This function will return the no. of days in that year.

SELECT
DAYOFYEAR('02-FEB-2021')
FROM DUAL;

Output:
33

6.9 STRING FUNCTIONS

These functions are used on input string and provide output in the required string format. String functions are applied on char data type and used to format the character sequence.

Some majorly used string functions in commonly used DBMSs are given below with suitable examples.

LENGTH(): Length function is used to count the no. of characters in a given string.

SELECT
LENGTH ("education")
FROM DUAL;

Output:
10

INSTR(): This function is used for finding the occurrence of a character in a given string.

SELECT
INSTR ("education", "u")
FROM DUAL;

Output:
3

LCASE(): This function is used to convert all characters into lower case of a given string.

SELECT
LCASE ("EDUCATION")
FROM DUAL;

Output:
education

UCASE(): This function is used to convert all characters into upper case of a given string.

SELECT
UCASE ("education")
FROM DUAL;

Output:
EDUCATION

SUBSTR(): This function is used to get a substring from a given string.

SELECT
UCASE ("education", 2,3)
FROM DUAL;

Output:
duc

LPAD(): This function is used to convert the given string into the required size by adding a special character in the left side.

SELECT
LPAD ("education", 12,' $')
FROM DUAL;

Output:
$$education

RPAD(): This function is used to convert the given string into the required size by adding a special character in the right side.

SELECT
RPAD ("education", 12,' $')
FROM DUAL;

Output:
education$$

6.10 CONVERSION FUNCTIONS

These conversion functions are used to convert one data type to other on retrieval of desired records. These are single row functions and used for type casting. Cross modification between date, number, and character is done using these functions.

There are three functions used for conversion [8, 9].

- TO_CHAR()

- TO_NUMBER()

- TO_DATE()

The working of these functions with an example is given below.

TO_CHAR(): This function is used for converting numeric or date data type to character data type. This conversion is done on the basis of the format given in function argument.

Syntax:
TO_CHAR(number1, [format], [nls_parameter])

The third parameter, i.e., nls_parameter is optional. It is used to specify the no. of decimal places, local currency label, etc.

Employee

Empno	Ename	Age	Sal	H_Date	Dept
101	Amit	38	2000	11-01-2009	10
102	Kabir	30	4500	13-04-1994	20
103	Monika	25	3000	02-04-2013	10
104	Kavita	35	3000	03-08-2020	30
105	Karan	34	5000	01-02-1998	30

Example: For example, we have used the above table

```
SELECT Ename,
TO_CHAR (H_Date, 'MON DD, YY') H_Date,
TO_CHAR (Sal, '$99999.99') Sal
FROM Employee
WHERE Age >30;
```

Output:

Employee

Ename	Sal	H_Date
Amit	$2000.00	Jan 11, 09
Kavita	$3000.00	Aug 03, 20
Karan	$5000.00	Feb 01, 98

TO_NUMBER(): This function is used for converting string or date data type to number data type. This conversion is done on the basis of the format given in function argument.

Syntax:
```
TO_NUMBER(string1, [format], [nls_parameter])
```

Example:
```
SELECT TO_NUMBER('2210.53', '9999.99')
FROM DUAL;
```

Output:
```
TO_NUMBER('2210.53', '9999.99')
-----------------------------
2210.53
```

TO_DATE(): This function is used for converting string type to date data type. This conversion is done on the basis of the format given in function argument.

Syntax:
TO_DATE(string1, [format], [nls_parameter])

Example:
SELECT TO_DATE(March 20, 2008, 10:00 P.M.', 'Month dd, YYYY, HH:MI P.M.', 'NLS_DATE_LANGUAGE=American')
FROM DUAL;

Output:
TO_DATE('

20-MAR-08

6.11 MATHEMATICAL FUNCTIONS

Mathematical functions are used to perform certain calculations on retrieved values. Using these functions in SQL queries, we can do some calculations on data.

Majorly used mathematical functions with their use and syntax are given below.

ABS(N): This function is used to find the absolute value of a given data item N.

Syntax:
SELECT
ABS(-15)
FROM DUAL;

Output:
15

MOD(M, N): In this function, M is divided by N, and the remainder will be given as the output.
SELECT
MOD(8,5)
FROM DUAL;

Output:
3

FLOOR(N): This function will return the smallest value that is near to N.
SELECT
FLOOR(7.6)
FROM DUAL;

Output:
7

CEIL(X): This function will return the largest value that is near to N.
SELECT
CEIL(7.6)
FROM DUAL;

Output:
8

POWER(X, Y): This function will return the value of X raised to the power Y.
SELECT
POWER(2,5)
FROM DUAL;

Output:
32

ROUND(X): This function returns an integer value nearest to the whole number X.
SELECT
ROUND(7.4)
FROM DUAL;

Output:
7

SQRT(X): This function will return the square root of X.
SELECT

SQRT(9)
FROM DUAL;

Output:
3

6.12 SPECIAL OPERATORS

There are some special operators in SQL used for specific functionalities. Some special operators are given below with their syntax and example.

- ALL

- ANY

- BETWEEN

- LIKE

- IN

The following table, named Employee, will be used for performing special operations.

Employee

Empno	Ename	Age	Sal	H_Date	Dept
101	Amit	38	2000	11-01-2009	10
102	Kabir	30	4500	13-04-1994	20
103	Monika	25	3000	02-04-2013	10
104	Kavita	35	3000	03-08-2020	30
105	Karan	34	5000	01-02-1998	30

ALL: This operator is used to compare all values returned from the sub-query and return only those rows for which the given condition satisfies for all values [10].

Select * from Employee
Where sal > ALL (select sal from Employee
where Deptno=10);
This query will return the records of all employees whose salary is greater than that of all employees working in department no. 10.

Employee					
Empno	Ename	Age	Sal	H_Date	Dept
102	Kabir	30	4500	13-04-1994	20
105	Karan	34	5000	01-02-1998	30

ANY: This operator is used to compare all values returned from the sub-query and returns only those rows for which the given condition satisfies for any of the returned values in the set of returned values [11, 12].

Select * from Employee
Where sal > ANY (select sal from Employee
where Deptno=10);

This query will return the records of all employees whose salary is greater than that of any employee working in department no. 10.

Output:

Employee					
Empno	Ename	Age	Sal	H_Date	Dept
102	Kabir	30	4500	13-04-1994	20
103	Monika	25	3000	02-04-2013	10
104	Kavita	35	3000	03-08-2020	30
105	Karan	34	5000	01-02-1998	30

BETWEEN: This operator is used to return the values in a given range. Minimum and maximum are given in query, and the records that satisfy the given range will be displayed.

Select * from Employee
Where sal BETWEEN 4000 AND 5000;

Output:

Employee					
Empno	Ename	Age	Sal	H_Date	Dept
102	Kabir	30	4500	13-04-1994	20
105	Karan	34	5000	01-02-1998	30

IN: This operator is used to return the values given in a particular list.
Select * from Employee
Where dept in (10,30);

Output:

Employee

Empno	Ename	Age	Sal	H_Date	Dept
101	Amit	38	2000	11-01-2009	10
103	Monika	25	3000	02-04-2013	10
104	Kavita	35	3000	03-08-2020	30
105	Karan	34	5000	01-02-1998	30

LIKE: This operator is used to return the values based upon some pattern matching in query.

Select * from Employee
Where ename like "K%";

Output:

Employee

Empno	Ename	Age	Sal	H_Date	Dept
102	Kabir	30	4500	13-04-1994	20
104	Kavita	35	3000	03-08-2020	30
105	Karan	34	5000	01-02-1998	30

6.13 TYPES OF CONSTRAINTS

SQL constraints are the set of rules applied on the columns of a table. These are used to provide restrictions on inserted values in applied columns of a table. These ensure the reliability and integrity of the data in respective columns.

There are majorly six types of constraints.

- **PRIMARY KEY**

- **UNIQUE**

- **NOT NULL**

- **FOREIGN KEY**
- **DEFAULT**
- **CHECK**

PRIMARY KEY: This constraint ensures or enforces to have unique and not-null values in each row of the applied column.

UNIQUE: This constraint ensures or enforces to have unique values in each row of the applied column. The constraint column may have null values, but if it has values, then they need to be unique.

NOT NULL: This constraint ensures or enforces to have not-null values in each row of the applied column. It enforces that some value needs to be inserted in this column if a record is inserted.

FOREIGN KEY: This constraint also ensures not-null values, but uniqueness may not be maintained. It is used to map between two tables. But it can have only those values that are mapped with the primary key column of other table.

DEFAULT: This constraint is used to insert a default value in the applied column if a value is not provided in the insert command.

CHECK: This constraint is used to maintain integrity of data in a table. This constraint is used to check the inserted value with the constrained value, and the record will be inserted only after satisfying the check constraint condition.

6.14 SUBQUERY

A subquery also called inner query is a nested query in which two or more SQL queries are embedded in each other. Whenever a SQL query is placed in where clause of some other SQL query than this concept is known a Subquery [4, 5].

This is used to return the data from one external query based on the output return by the internal query. A subquery can be used with SELECT, UPDATE, DELETE, and INSERT command with SQL operators including <, >, =, <=, BETWEEN, IN, ANY, ALL EXIST, etc.

There are some set of rules to be followed before writing a subquery.

- It must be enclosed in parentheses.

- ORDER BY clause should not use in subquery. ORDER BY clause can be used in main query.

- The inner query should return a single column until multiple columns are not compared in the main query.

- IN operator can be used if multiple rows are returned by the inner query.

- BETWEEN operator can be used in inner query, but it cannot be used in main query.

Syntax:
The syntax for SELECT subquery is given below
SELECT col_name
FROM Tab_name
WHERE col_name OPERATOR
(
SELECT col_name
FROM Tab_name
WHERE col_name
)

Example: If we execute the following subquery on our Employee table, then we will have the following output.

SELECT Empno, Ename
FROM Employee
WHERE sal =
(
SELECT max(sal)
FROM Employee
)

Output:

Employee	
Empno	Ename
105	Karan

6.15 SUMMARY

SQL is a standard query language used by a relational database for creating, inserting, and modifying information in its database. SQL is a very flexible programming language. It follow ANSI standard. The command used in SQL is divided into four major categories including DDL, DML, DCL, TCL, and DQL. There are many operations used in SQL to retrieve the required results. There are many types of functions available for a specific task including mathematical function, which can be used to perform calculation on data, string functions, which can be used for manipulation of string format, and data functions, which are used for changing date format and do some calculation of date columns. The constraints available in SQL are used to ensure relevant values in attributes. Subqueries can be used for embedding a query inside a query to find results that are more complex.

6.16 REVIEW QUESTIONS

1. What is SQL (Structured Query Language)? What are the advantages of SQL?

2. Write a short note on the following

    a. Data Definition Language (DDL)

    b. Data Manipulation Language (DML)

3. What is SQL constraint? Explain the different types of SQL constraints.

4. What is the significance of a mathematical operator in SQL? Explain with an example.

5. What is subquery? What is the significance of subquery in SQL?

6. What is the difference between primary key and foreign key constraint?

7. Explain the following operators with an example.

    a. ANY

    b. ALL

    c. IN

    d. BETWEEN

8. Using subquery in following table, write the query to retrieve all employee records whose salary is less than the maximum salary.

Employee					
Empno	Ename	Age	Sal	H_Date	Dept
101	Amit	38	2000	11-01-2009	10
102	Kabir	30	4500	13-04-1994	20
103	Monika	25	3000	02-04-2013	10
104	Kavita	35	3000	03-08-2020	30
105	Karan	34	5000	01-02-1998	30

9. Write a query on the above employee table to retrieve records of all employees whose names are starting with letter "K".

10. Write a query on the above table to print the Hire Date column in "DD-MONTH-YYYY" format.

REFERENCES

1. K. Dias, M. Ramacher, U. Shaft, and G. Wood, "Automatic Performance Diagnosis and Tuning in Oracle," Proceedings of CIDR, pp. 1110–1121, 2005.
2. K. P. Brown, M. J. Carey, and M. Livny, "Goal-Oriented Buffer Management Revisited," Proceedings of ACM SIGMOD Conference, Montreal, pp. 353–364, 1996.
3. K. P. Brown, M. J. Carey, and M. Livny, Towards an Autopilot in the DBMS Performance Cockpit, High Performance Transaction Systems Workshop, 1993.
4. K. P. Brown, M. Mehta, M. J. Carey, and M. Livny (1994) Towards Automated Performance Tuning For Complex Workloads, Proceedings of the 20th International VLDB Conference, pp. 72–84, Santiago, Chile.
5. H. K. Sharma, S. Kumar, S. Dubey, P. Gupta, "Auto-selection and management of dynamic SGA Parameters in RDBMS," International Conference on Computing for Sustainable Global Development, INDIACom, pp. 1763–1768, 2015.
6. H. K. Sharma and M. S. C. Nelson, "Performance enhancement using SQL statement tuning approach", Database Systems Journal, vol. 8, no. 1, pp. 12–21.
7. A. Shastri, R. Biswas, and S. K. Singh, "SGA Dynamic Parameters: The Core Components of Automated Database Tuning", Database Systems Journal, vol. 5, no. 2, pp. 13–21.
8. M. S. C. Nelson, "Explain Plan and SQL Trace the Two Approaches for RDBMS Tuning", Database Systems Journal, vol. 8, no. 1, pp. 31–39.

9. H. K. Sharma and S. K. Singh, "Tuning I/O Subsystem: A Key Component in RDBMS Performance Tuning", *Database Systems Journal*, vol. 7, no. 1, 3–11.

10. H. K. Sharma, A. Shastri, and R. Biswas, "An Algorithmic Approach for Auto-Selection of Resources to Self-Tune the Database", *IJRIT International Journal of Research in Information Technology*, vol. 1, no. 9, pp. 288–289.

11. H. K. Sharma, A. Shastri, and R. Biswas, "ARH_Db_Tuner The GUI tool to Monitor and Diagnose the SGA Parameters Automatically", *Database Systems Journal*, vol. 4, no. 1.

12. R. Biswas, "A Framework for Automated Database TuningUsing Dynamic SGA Parameters and Basic Operating System Utilities", *Database System Journal Romania*, 2013.

13. Dynamic Reconfiguration: Dynamically Tuning Multiple Buffer Pools, Proceedings of the International Conference on Database and Expert System Applications (DEXA'2000), pp. 92–101.

CHAPTER 7

Introduction to PL/SQL

As we have learnt so far about SQL, SQL stands for structured query language, i.e., used to perform operations on the records stored in a database such as inserting records, updating records, deleting records, creating, modifying and dropping tables, and views. The extension to SQL to make more manageable and independent code is called PL/SQL, i.e., procedural language extension of SQL.

PL/SQL is a block structured language that can have multiple blocks in it. This chapter discusses about the conditional statements, loops, arrays, string, exceptions, collections, records, triggers, functions, procedures, and cursors in PL/SQL.

7.1 PL/SQL

The PL/SQL includes the functionalities provided by most of the programming languages such as declaring variables, constants, conditional statements, and loops and furthermore also supports triggers. Advanced techniques such as exception handling and array data structure are also supported. In later version of Oracle, even object-oriented features are made available to PL/SQL. The important thing to know and remember about PL/SQL is that these programs are stored and executed on DBMS only. They can be triggered based upon change in value on tables. This helps in processing the data in near real time on the database itself.

Unlike other procedural language, PL/SQL is not case-sensitive, and you can use any combination of lower case and upper case letters. The lexical units composed of characters in a line of PL/SQL text can be classified into delimiters, identifiers, literals, and comments.

DOI: 10.1201/9780429282843-7

7.2 VARIABLES AND CONSTANTS

Similar to other programming languages, PL/SQL also uses variables to store temporary state of the program. In other words, we can say that variable is a meaningful name given to the storage memory. Variables are used to manipulate the data during the execution of the program. The variables have a data type and size that define what kind of data and how much data can be stored inside one variable. Few points to remember about variables:

- The naming rule states that the name of a variable should not exceed 30 characters.

- The first letter should be any letter only, followed by any alphanumeric, dollar sign, and underscore.

- The dollar sign and underscore are provided to create readability in the long variable name.

- The variable names are not case-sensitive.

- The variable should be declared in the declaration section of PL/SQL block.

- A reserved PL/SQL keyword cannot be used as a variable name.

- NOT NULL is an optional specification on the variable.

The variable is defined in the declaration section of the program. The variable by default comprises a NULL value, and to initialize it with some initial value, we can either use the assignment operator (:=) or DEFAULT keyword. The syntax with example is shown below.

```
variableName DataType := initial_Value
for e.g., salary intger:=20000
or
variableName DataType DEFAULT initial_Value
for e.g., salary integer DEFAULT 20000
```

The PL/SQL allows nesting of blocks. A program block can contain another inner block. If you declare a variable within an inner block, it is not accessible to an outer block. There are two types of variable scope:

- Local Variable: Local variables are the inner block variables which are not accessible to outer blocks.

- Global Variable: Global variables are declared in the outermost block.

7.2.1 Constant

The constants are special identifiers whose value does not change once specified. The special keyword CONSTANT is written after the identifiers name to make it constant. For example:

PI CONSTANT real:=3.14

7.3 DATA TYPES

Predefined PL/SQL datatypes are grouped into composite, LOB, reference, and scalar-type categories.

- A composite type has internal components that can be manipulated individually, such as the elements of an array, record, or table.

- A LOB type holds values, called lob locators, that specify the location of large objects, such as text blocks or graphic images, that are stored separately from other database data. LOB types include BFILE, BLOB, CLOB, and NCLOB [1].

- A reference type holds values, called pointers, that designate other program items. These types include REF CURSORS and REFs to object types [2].

- A scalar type has no internal components. It holds a single value, such as a number or character string. The scalar types fall into four families, which store number, character, Boolean, and date/time data. The scalar families with their datatypes are as follows.

7.3.1 PL/SQL Number Types [3]

BINARY_DOUBLE, BINARY_FLOAT, BINARY_INTEGER, DEC, DECIMAL, DOUBLE PRECISION, FLOAT, INT, INTEGER, NATURAL, NATURALN, NUMBER, NUMERIC, PLS_INTEGER, POSITIVE, POSITIVEN, REAL, SIGNTYPE, SMALLINT

7.3.2 PL/SQL Character and String Types and PL/SQL National Character Types

CHAR, CHARACTER, LONG, LONG RAW, NCHAR, NVARCHAR2, RAW, ROWID, STRING, UROWID, VARCHAR, VARCHAR2

7.3.3 "LONG and LONG RAW Datatypes"

The LONG and LONG RAW datatypes are supported only for backward compatibility.

7.3.4 PL/SQL Date, Time, and Interval Types

DATE, TIMESTAMP, TIMESTAMP WITH TIMEZONE, TIMESTAMP WITH LOCAL TIMEZONE, INTERVAL YEAR TO MONTH, INTERVAL DAY TOSECOND (Figure 7.1).

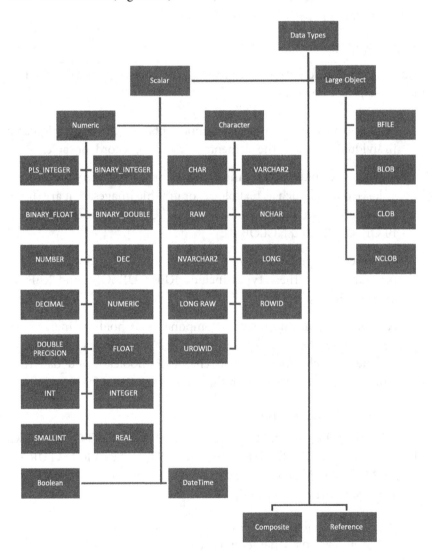

FIGURE 7.1   Data types in PL/SQL.

7.3.5 NULLs in PL/SQL

PL/SQL NULL values represent **missing** or **unknown data,** and they are not an integer, a character, or any other specific data type. Note that **NULL** is not the same as an empty data string or the null character value '\0'. A null can be assigned, but it cannot be equated with anything, including itself.

7.4 PL/SQL LITERALS

Literals are the explicit numeric, character, string, or Boolean values, which are not represented by an identifier. For example, TRUE and NULL are all literals of type Boolean. PL/SQL literals are case-sensitive. There are the following kinds of literals in PL/SQL:

- Numeric Literals

- Character Literals

- String Literals

- BOOLEAN Literals

- Date and Time Literals

7.4.1 Example of These Different Types of Literals

Literals	Examples
Numeric	75125, 3568, 33.3333333, etc.
Character	'A' '%' '9' '' 'z' '(' '
String	Hello JavaTpoint!
Boolean	TRUE, FALSE, NULL, etc.
Date and Time	'26-11-2002', '2012-10-29 12:01:01'

7.5 CONTROL STATEMENTS

Most of the time in any procedural program, we encounter the situation where some decision needs to be taken before executing the next statement and/or the need of repetition of code is there. Almost every programming language supports conditional statements and loop statements. Similarly, PL/SQL also supports the programming language features like conditional statements and iterative statements. The syntax is very similar to any other procedural language.

7.5.1 If Statement

If is used for conditional statements, where we can define multiple blocks in the code that executes based upon conditions. If statements can be classified into different types based upon requirements. All if statements take a Boolean condition, and based upon its evaluation, the required block gets executed.

7.5.1.1 IF-THEN Statement

It is used when one statement or block needs to be executed based on one condition only.

1. IF condition

2. THEN

3. Statement: {It is executed when the condition is true}

4. END IF;

7.5.1.2 IF-THEN-ELSE Statement

Used when two statements or block needs to be executed based on one condition only.

1. IF condition

2. THEN

3. {...statements to execute when the condition is TRUE...}

4. ELSE

5. {...statements to execute when the condition is FALSE...}

6. END IF;

Syntax: (IF-THEN-ELSIF statement): Also called as elsif ladder, this is used when multiple statements or block needs to be executed based on multiple conditions.

1. IF condition1

2. THEN

3. {...statements to execute when condition1 is TRUE...}

4. ELSIF condition2

5. THEN

6. {...statements to execute when condition2 is TRUE...}

7. END IF;

Syntax: (IF-THEN-ELSIF-ELSE statement): This is used when multiple statements or block needs to be executed based on multiple conditions, and there is one last condition that executes if all previously provided conditions are false.

1. IF condition1

2. THEN

3. {...statements to execute when condition1 is TRUE...}

4. ELSIF condition2

5. THEN

6. {...statements to execute when condition2 is TRUE...}

7. ELSE

8. {...statements to execute when both condition1 and condition2 are FALSE...}

9. END IF;

7.5.2 Example of PL/SQL If Statement
Let's take an example to see the whole concept:

1. DECLARE

2. ram_age number(2) := 26;

3. BEGIN

4. --check for ram age to be eligible for voting

5. IF(ram_age < 18) THEN

6. –if ram_age is less than 18

7. dbms_output.put_line('Not eligible to vote');

8. ELSE

9. dbms_output.put_line('Eligible to Vote');

10. END IF;

11. dbms_output.put_line('The age is: ' || ram_age);

12. END;

After the execution of the above code in SQL prompt, you will get the following result:

Eligible to Vote
The age is: 26
PL/SQL procedure successfully completed.

7.6 PL/SQL CASE STATEMENT

The case statements are similar to switch case in procedural languages. The CASE statement in PL/SQL are used when there are many alternate conditions and the comparison needs to make is "equality".

The "CASE" statement takes the expression and evaluates it against provided "WHEN" conditions. Whenever a case expression is matched with WHEN, it executes the corresponding THEN part and ignores the other. If there is no WHEN part matched in that case, the ELSE part is executed.

Syntax for the CASE Statement

1. CASE [expression]

2. WHEN condition_1 THEN result_1

3. WHEN condition_2 THEN result_2

4. ...

5. WHEN condition_n THEN result_n

6. ELSE result

7. END

7.6.1 Example of PL/SQL Case Statement

Let's take an example to make it clear:

1. DECLARE

2. day number(1) := 2;

3. BEGIN

4. CASE day

5. when 1 then dbms_output.put_line(Sunday);

6. when 2 then dbms_output.put_line(Monday);

7. when 3 then dbms_output.put_line(Tuesday);

8. when 4 then dbms_output.put_line(Wednesday);

9. when 5 then dbms_output.put_line('Thursday');

10. when 6 then dbms_output.put_line('Friday');

11. when 7 then dbms_output.put_line('Saturday');

12. else dbms_output.put_line(Invalid Day);

13. END CASE;

14. END;

After the execution of the above code, you will get the following result:
Monday
PL/SQL procedure successfully completed.

7.7 PL/SQL LOOP

The PL/SQL loops are used when a block of statement is required to be repeated several times. Generally, the loop will have a control variable that contains the initial value, a termination condition, and an expression that changes the control variable.

Without specifying the termination condition, we may lead the loop to infinite condition. PL/SQL features four types of loops.

1. Basic Loop/Exit Loop

2. While Loop

3. For Loop

4. Cursor For Loop

Syntax: (Basic Loop/Exit Loop): This type of loop consists of an exit condition that terminates the loop. If the termination condition is not specified, then the loop becomes infinite loop.

1. LOOP

2. statements;

3. EXIT;

4. {or EXIT **WHEN** condition;}

5. **END** LOOP;

The following points need to be considered while creating the loop:

- Initialize a variable before the loop body.

- Increment the variable in the loop.

- You should use EXIT with the WHEN or IF statement as demonstrated in the examples below.

7.7.1 Example of PL/SQL EXIT Loop with WHEN Condition

Let's take a simple example to explain it well:

1. DECLARE

2. i NUMBER := 2;

3. BEGIN

4. LOOP

5. EXIT **WHEN** i>20;

6. DBMS_OUTPUT.PUT_LINE(i);

7. i := i+2;

8. **END** LOOP;

9. **END**;

After the execution of the above code, you will get the following result:

Output:

2

4

6

8

10

12

14

16

18

20

7.8 PL/SQL EXIT LOOP EXAMPLE WITH IF CONDITION

1. DECLARE

2. x NUMBER;

3. y NUMBER;

4. BEGIN

5. x:=10;

6. y:=1;

7. LOOP

8. DBMS_OUTPUT.PUT_LINE (x*y);

9. IF (y=10) **THEN**

10. EXIT;

11. **END** IF;

12. y:=y+1;

13. **END** LOOP;

14. **END**;

Output:

10

20

30

40

50

60

70

80

90

100

Syntax: (While Loop): This type of loop starts with a condition, and the condition is checked before execution of the first statement. The statement repeats itself until the condition is true.

Syntax of while loop:

1. WHILE <condition>

2. LOOP statements;

3. END LOOP;

The following points need to be considered while creating the while loop:

- Initialize a variable before the loop body.

- Increment the variable in the loop.

- Usage of EXIT with the WHEN or IF statement is optional in while loop.

7.8.1 Example of PL/SQL While Loop

Let's see a simple example of PL/SQL WHILE loop.

1. DECLARE

2. i **INTEGER** := 2;

3. BEGIN

4. WHILE i <= 20 LOOP

5. DBMS_OUTPUT.PUT_LINE(i);

6. i := i+2;

7. **END** LOOP;

8. **END**;

After the execution of the above code, you will get the following result:
Output:
2
4
6
8
10
12
14
16
18
20

7.8.2 PL/SQL WHILE Loop Example 2

1. DECLARE

2. x NUMBER;

3. y NUMBER;

4. BEGIN

5. x:=10;

6. y:=1;

7. WHILE (y<=10)

8. LOOP

9. DBMS_OUTPUT.PUT_LINE (x*y);

10. y:=y+1;

11. **END** LOOP;

12. **END**;

Output:
    10
    20
    30
    40
    50
    60
    70
    80
    90
    100

Syntax: (FOR Loop): This type of loop is most preferred because of its simplicity. The loop automatically iterates between the initial and final value. The only point to remember is that this is used only for incrementing the value by 1.

    1. **FOR** counter IN initial_value.. final_value LOOP

    2. LOOP statements;

    3. **END** LOOP;

Where,
    initial_value: Start integer value
    final_value: End integer value
    The following points need to be considered while creating the while loop:

- Counter variable is not required to be created, it is automatically created.

- The counter variable is always incremented by 1.

- Usage of EXIT with the WHEN or IF statement is optional in while loop.

7.8.3 PL/SQL for Loop Example 1

Let's see a simple example of PL/SQL FOR loop.

    1. BEGIN

    2. **FOR** i IN 1..5 LOOP

3. DBMS_OUTPUT.PUT_LINE(i);

4. **END** LOOP;

5. **END**;

Output:
1
2
3
4
5

7.8.4 PL/SQL for Loop REVERSE Example

Let's see an example of PL/SQL for loop where we are using REVERSE keyword.

1. DECLARE

2. x NUMBER;

3. BEGIN

4. x:=10;

5. FOR i IN REVERSE 1..10

6. LOOP

7. DBMS_OUTPUT.PUT_LINE (x*i);

8. END LOOP;

9. END;

Output:
100
90
80
70
60
50
40
30

20
10

7.9 PL/SQL CONTINUE STATEMENT

The continue statement is similar to the continue statement in procedural languages. The control skips all the statements that follow the continue statement in the loop and start iterating from the entry of loop. The continue statement is introduced in Oracle11g version and depends on the DBMS for its support.

7.9.1 Example of PL/SQL Continue Statement

Let's take an example of PL/SQL continue statement.

1. DECLARE

2. x NUMBER := 0;

3. BEGIN

4. LOOP – Entry point of loop

5. DBMS_OUTPUT.PUT_LINE (Inner loop: x=' || TO_CHAR(x));

6. x := x+1;

7. IF x<3 THEN

8. CONTINUE;

9. END IF;

10. DBMS_OUTPUT.PUT_LINE

11. (Inner loop, after CONTINUE: x=' || TO_CHAR(x));

12. EXIT WHEN x=5;

13. END LOOP;

14. DBMS_OUTPUT.PUT_LINE (' After loop: x=' || TO_CHAR(x));

15. END;

After the execution of the above code, you will get the following result:
  Inner loop: x=0
  Inner loop: x=1

Inner loop: x=2
Inner loop, after CONTINUE: x=3
Inner loop: x=3
Inner loop, after CONTINUE: x=4
Inner loop: x=4
Inner loop, after CONTINUE: x=5
After loop: x=5

7.10 PL/SQL GOTO STATEMENT

The GOTO statement can take control of any specified label within the
subprogram. The GOTO statement needs a label to define where to jump,
and the label name can be defined between << and >>. The label name
should have at least one statement following.

Syntax for GOTO:

1. GOTO label_name;

Syntax for label name:

1. <<label_name>>

The following points need to be considered while using the GOTO
statement:

- GOTO cannot be used to transfer control into/from an IF statement,
  CASE statement, LOOP statement, or subblock.

- GOTO cannot transfer control from an outer block into a subblock.

- GOTO cannot transfer control out of a subprogram.

- GOTO cannot transfer control into an exception handler.

7.10.1 Example of PL/SQL GOTO Statement

Let's take an example of the PL/SQL GOTO statement.

1. DECLARE

2. a number(2) := 30;

3. BEGIN

4. <<customlabel>>

5. WHILE a<41 LOOP

6. dbms_output.put_line ('value of a:' || a);

7. a := a+1;

8. IF a=35 THEN

9. a := a+1;

10. GOTO customlabel;

11. END IF;

12. END LOOP;

13. END;

Output:
    value of a: 30
    value of a: 31
    value of a: 32
    value of a: 33
    value of a: 34
    value of a: 36
    value of a: 37
    value of a: 38
    value of a: 39
    value of a: 40
    Statement processed.

7.11 PL/SQL PROCEDURE AND FUNCTIONS

The PL/SQL procedures and functions are the main application of PL/SQL; the procedures and functions are stored on a DBMS server and can be triggered manually or automatically. The use of procedures and functions in a DBMS reduces the workload on business application for intermediate processing of data. The procedures and functions are named methods _containing the block. The procedure and function comprise header and body. The header section contains the name and parameters for the procedure or function. The body section contains the executable PL/SQL block. Both procedures and functions can have three types of parameters as explained below.

1. **IN parameters:** The IN parameters are those read-only variables that can be referenced by the procedure or function but cannot be changed.

2. **OUT parameters:** The OUT parameters are those variables that can be referenced by the procedure or function and can be changed.

3. **INOUT parameters:** The INOUT parameters are those variables that can be referenced in read and write mode by the procedure or function.

The main and only difference between the procedures and functions is that the procedure may or may not return a value, whereas a function must return a value.

The following subsections explain the syntax with examples of procedures and functions.

7.11.1 PL/SQL Procedure Syntax and Examples

Syntax for creating procedure:

1. CREATE [OR REPLACE] PROCEDURE procedure_name

2. [parameter_name TYPE DataType]

3. IS

4. [declaration_section]

5. BEGIN

6. executable_section

7. [EXCEPTION

8. exception_section]

9. END [procedure_name];

7.11.1.1 PL/SQL Procedure Example

This example demonstrates the complete process to create, call, and delete a procedure. The example creates a procedure to insert employee in EMPLOYEE table, and the code below creates an EMPLOYEE table followed by creating a procedure and then calling it in other PL/SQL block and finally deleting the procedure.

Table Creation:

1. create table EMPLOYEE(eid number(10) primary key, name varchar2(100));

Procedure Code:

1. create or replace procedure "insertEmployee"

2. (eid IN NUMBER,

3. name IN VARCHAR2)

4. IS

5. BEGIN

6. insert into user values(id, name);

7. end;

Calling the Procedure in PL/SQL code:

1. BEGIN

2. insertEmployee (101, 'Einstein');

3. dbms_output.put_line('record inserted successfully');

4. END;

Now, see the "EMPLOYEE" table; you will see that one record is inserted.

EID	Name
101	Einstein

DROP the Procedure Syntax:

1. DROP PROCEDURE procedure_name;

Example of drop procedure

1. DROP PROCEDURE insertEmployee;

7.11.2 PL/SQL Function Syntax and Examples
Syntax to create a function:

1. CREATE [OR REPLACE] FUNCTION function_name [parameters]

2. [(parameter_name [IN | OUT | IN OUT] type [,...])]

3. RETURN return_datatype

4. {IS | AS}

5. BEGIN

6. < function_body >

7. END [function_name];

Note: The function must contain a return statement.

- RETURN clause specifies the data type you are going to return from the function.

- Function_body contains the executable part.

- The AS keyword is used instead of the IS keyword for creating a standalone function.

7.11.2.1 PL/SQL Function Example
This example demonstrates the complete process to create, call, and delete a procedure. The example creates a function to do addition of two numbers. The code below creates a procedure and then calling it in other PL/SQL block and finally deleting the procedure.
Function Code:

1. create or replace function sumFun(x IN number, y IN number)

2. return number

3. IS

4. result number(8);

5. BEGIN

6. result :=x+y;

7. return result;

8. END;

Calling the Function in PL/SQL code:

1. DECLARE

2. result number(2);

3. BEGIN

4. result := sumFun(10,20);

5. dbms_output.put_line('Addition is:' || result);

6. END;

Output:
Addition is: 30
Statement processed.
0.05 seconds
DROP the Function Syntax:

1. DROP PROCEDURE function_name;

Example of DROP Function.

2. DROP PROCEDURE sumFun;

PL/SQL Function Example 2
This example demonstrates the function that can find a maximum of two numbers. The example consists of defining function and calling in the same code.

1. DECLARE

2. x number;

3. y number;

4. z number;

5. FUNCTION findMax(a IN number, b IN number)

6. RETURN number

7. IS

8. c number;

9. BEGIN

10. IF a>b THEN

11. c:= a;

12. ELSE

13. c:= y;

14. END IF;

15. RETURN c;

16. END;

17. BEGIN

18. x:= 50;

19. y:= 60;

20. 20.

21. z := findMax(x, y);

22. dbms_output.put_line('Maximum is:' || z);

23. END;

Output:
Maximum is: 60
Statement processed.
0.02 seconds

7.11.2.2 PL/SQL Function Example 3
This example demonstrates the usage of SQL syntax in function and returning the result. The Employee table is taken for better understanding of the code. The function will return the total number of employees in the table.

Employee

Id	Name
1	Eric
2	Ted
3	Bob
4	Alice

Function Code:

1. CREATE OR REPLACE FUNCTION employeeCount

2. RETURN number IS

3. result number(2) := 0;

4. BEGIN

5. SELECT count(*) into result

6. FROM Employee;

7. RETURN result;

8. END;

After the execution of the above code, you will get the following result.
Function created.
Calling the Function in PL/SQL code:

1. DECLARE

2. result number(2);

3. BEGIN

4. result := employeeCount();

5. dbms_output.put_line('Total no. of Employee:' || result);

6. END;

After the execution of the above code in SQL prompt, you will get the following result.

Total no. of Employee: 4
PL/SQL procedure successfully completed.

7.11.2.3 PL/SQL Function Example 4

This example demonstrated the recursive functions in PL/SQL to calculate the factorial of a given number. The recursive functions are functions that call themselves. There needs to be a termination condition to stop the recursion. In this case, the termination condition is that the factorial of 1 is always 1.

```
1. DECLARE
2. ip number;
3. fact number;
4. FUNCTION factorial(x number)
5. RETURN number
6. IS
7. f number;
8. BEGIN
9. IF x=1 THEN
10. f := 1;
11. ELSE
12. f := x * factorial(x-1);
13. END IF;
14. RETURN f;
15. END;
16. BEGIN
17. ip:= 5;
18. fact := factorial(ip);
19. dbms_output.put_line('Factorial '|| ip || ' is ' || fact);
20. END;
```

After the execution of the above code at SQL prompt, it produces the following result.

Factorial 5 is 120

PL/SQL procedure successfully completed.

7.12 PL/SQL CURSOR

The part of the memory where the process statements are stored is known as context memory. This memory contains all intermediate results, and this can be used for more optimized query. To access this memory location, a cursor is used, and the cursor can be resembled to pointers in some procedural language. The cursor contains the information on a select statement and the rows of data accessed by it. Further, cursor contains attributes that can be used in PL/SQL statements. The cursors are of two types:

1. Implicit Cursors

2. Explicit Cursors

7.12.1 PL/SQL Implicit Cursors

As the name states, the implicit cursors are generated automatically when an SQL statement is executed. They are generated for all DML statements. Some of the attributes that are provided by DBMS are %FOUND, %NOTFOUND, %ROWCOUNT, and %ISOPEN.

The following table specifies the status of the cursor with each of its attribute.

Attribute	Description
%FOUND	Its return value is TRUE if DML statements like INSERT, DELETE, and UPDATE affect at least one row or more rows or a SELECT INTO statement returned one or more rows. Otherwise it returns FALSE.
%NOTFOUND	Its return value is TRUE if DML statements like INSERT, DELETE, and UPDATE affect no row, or a SELECT INTO statement returns no rows. Otherwise it returns FALSE. It is just the opposite of %FOUND.
%ISOPEN	It always returns FALSE for implicit cursors, because the SQL cursor is automatically closed after executing its associated SQL statements.
%ROWCOUNT	It returns the number of rows affected by DML statements like INSERT, DELETE, and UPDATE or returned by a SELECT INTO statement.

7.12.2 PL/SQL Implicit Cursor Example

This example demonstrates the use of SQL%ROWCOUNT attribute. The table given below is used to understand the outcome.

Create Employee table and have records:

ID	NAME	AGE	ADDRESS	SALARY
1	Alice	22	California	20000
2	Bob	23	NY	22000
3	Mark	21	Georgia	24000
4	Steven	29	California	26000
5	Jack	22	Texas	28000

1. DECLARE

2. rows number(2);

3. BEGIN

4. UPDATE Employee

5. SET salary=salary+5000;

6. IF sql%notfound THEN

7. dbms_output.put_line('no Employee updated');

8. ELSIF sql%found THEN

9. rows := sql%rowcount;

10. dbms_output.put_line(rows || ' Employees updated ');

11. END IF;

12. END;

Output:
  5 Employees updated
  PL/SQL procedure successfully completed.

7.12.3 PL/SQL Explicit Cursors

The explicit cursors are defined in the PL/SQL block by the programmer to utilize the benefits of the context area. It is created on a SELECT statement which returns more than one row.

Following are the typical steps using the explicit cursor:

1. Declare the cursor to initialize in the memory.

2. Open the cursor to allocate memory.

3. Fetch the cursor to retrieve data.

4. Close the cursor to release allocated memory.

- Syntax to declare a cursor:

  1. CURSOR name IS

  2. **SELECT** statement;

- Syntax to open a cursor

  1. **OPEN** cursor_name;

- Syntax to fetch a cursor

  1. **FETCH** cursor_name **INTO** variable_list;

- Syntax to close a cursor

  1. **Close** cursor_name;

7.12.3.1 PL/SQL Explicit Cursor Example
This example demonstrates the use of declare open fetch and close an explicit cursor. The table given below is used to understand the outcome. Observe the usage of implicit cursor in line 11.
Create Employee table and have records:

ID	NAME	AGE	ADDRESS	SALARY
1	Alice	22	California	20000
2	Bob	23	NY	22000
3	Mark	21	Georgia	24000
4	Steven	29	California	26000
5	Jack	22	Texas	28000

Execute the following program to retrieve the employee name and address.

1. DECLARE

2. e_id empoyee.id%type;

3. e_name employee.**name**%type;

4. e_addr employee.address%type;

5. **CURSOR** cursor_employee **is**

6. **SELECT** id, **name**, address **FROM** employee;

7. BEGIN

8. **OPEN** cursor_employee;

9. LOOP

10. **FETCH** cursor_employee **into** e_id, e_name, e_addr;

11. EXIT **WHEN** cursor_employee %notfound;

12. dbms_output.put_line(e_id || ' ' || e_name || ' ' || e_addr);

13. **END** LOOP;

14. **CLOSE** cursor_employee;

15. **END**;

Output:

1. Alice California

2. Bob NY

3. Mark Georgia

4. Steven California

5. Jack Texas

PL/SQL procedure successfully completed.

7.13 PL/SQL EXCEPTION

An error occurring during the program execution is called exception in PL/SQL.

PL/SQL facilitates programmers to catch such conditions using exception block in the program, and an appropriate action is taken against the error condition.

There are two types of exceptions:

- System-defined exceptions

- User-defined exceptions

7.14 PL/SQL EXCEPTION HANDLING

The abnormality occurring in a program during execution due to logical or any other type of error is termed the exception. The exception ultimately leads to error and terminates the program, for e.g., if no matching record is found in a table.

The mechanism to make program robust in case of such exception is called as exception handling. PL/SQL helps in exception handling by providing the exception block; this helps in providing appropriate fail-safe mechanism to gracefully execute or terminate the program in case of abnormality.

Syntax for Exception Handling

Following is a general syntax for exception handling; look carefully for EXCEPTION block and WHEN conditions.

1. DECLARE

2. <declarations **section**>

3. BEGIN

4. <executable command(s)>

5. EXCEPTION

6. <exception handling goes here >

7. **WHEN** exception1 **THEN**

8. exception1-handling-statements

9. **WHEN** exception2 **THEN**

10. exception2-handling-statements

11. **WHEN** exception3 **THEN**

12. exception3-handling-statements

13. ....

14. **WHEN** others **THEN**

15. exception3-handling-statements

16. **END**;

There are two types of exceptions:

- System-defined exceptions
  - These are the known exceptions that are automatically raised by the database server.
- User-defined exceptions
  - While writing the custom logic, the programmer may also define exceptions for robust program; these exceptions are called user-defined exceptions. These exceptions need to be raised manually.

Let us first understand the exception handling by a simple example; note that the exceptions are automatically raised in the program below and are system-defined exceptions.

7.14.1 System-Defined Exception Handling

Let's take a simple example to demonstrate the concept of exception handling. Here we are using the already created employee table. The e_id variable is initialized with 6; note that 6 does not exist in our table. This raises an exception in the program. Using the Exception block, we catch this and gracefully print a graceful message to the user.

SELECT* FROM Employee;

ID	NAME	AGE	ADDRESS	SALARY
1	Alice	22	California	20000
2	Bob	23	NY	22000
3	Mark	21	Georgia	24000
4	Steven	29	California	26000
5	Jack	22	Texas	28000

1. DECLARE

2. e_id employee.id%type := 6;

3. e_name employee.**name**%type;

4. e_addr employee.address%type;

5. BEGIN

6. **SELECT name**, address **INTO** e_name, e_addr

7. **FROM** employee

8. **WHERE** id = e_id;

9. DBMS_OUTPUT.PUT_LINE ('Name: '|| c_name);

10. DBMS_OUTPUT.PUT_LINE ('Address: ' || c_addr);

11. EXCEPTION

12. **WHEN** no_data_found **THEN**

13. dbms_output.put_line('No such customer!');

14. **WHEN** others **THEN**

15. dbms_output.put_line('Error!');

16. **END**;

Output of the above code:
No such customer!
PL/SQL procedure successfully completed.
In the same example, if we set e_id to any value between 1 and 5, we will get correct output. For e.g., let e_id:=4, the output would be as follows:
Name: Steven
Address: California
PL/SQL procedure successfully completed.

7.14.2 System-Defined Exceptions
We have seen how an exception handling is done; again in the above example, one should observe that the exception was raised automatically by the database system and was a system-defined exception. There are many predefined exceptions in PL/SQL, which are executed when any database rule is violated by the programs.

The below table presents some of the predefined exceptions:

Exception	Oracle Error	SQL Code	Description
ACCESS_INTO_NULL	06530	−6530	It is raised when a NULL object is automatically assigned a value.
CASE_NOT_FOUND	06592	−6592	It is raised when none of the choices in the "WHEN" clauses of a CASE statement is selected, and there is no else clause.
COLLECTION_IS_NULL	06531	−6531	It is raised when a program attempts to apply collection methods other than that exists to an uninitialized nested table or varray, or the program attempts to assign values to the elements of an uninitialized nested table or varray.
DUP_VAL_ON_INDEX	00001	−1	It is raised when duplicate values are attempted to be stored in a column with unique index.
INVALID_CURSOR	01001	−1001	It is raised when attempts are made to make a cursor operation that is not allowed, such as closing an unopened cursor.
INVALID_NUMBER	01722	−1722	It is raised when the conversion of a character string into a number fails because the string does not represent a valid number.
LOGIN_DENIED	01017	−1017	It is raised when a program attempts to log on to the database with an invalid username or password.
NO_DATA_FOUND	01403	+100	It is raised when a select into statement returns no rows.
NOT_LOGGED_ON	01012	−1012	It is raised when a database call is issued without being connected to the database.
PROGRAM_ERROR	06501	−6501	It is raised when PL/SQL has an internal problem.
ROWTYPE_MISMATCH	06504	−6504	It is raised when a cursor fetches value in a variable having incompatible data type.
SELF_IS_NULL	30625	−30625	It is raised when a member method is invoked, but the instance of the object type is not initialized.
STORAGE_ERROR	06500	−6500	It is raised when PL/SQL runs out of memory or memory is corrupted.
TOO_MANY_ROWS	01422	−1422	It is raised when a SELECT INTO statement returns more than one row.
VALUE_ERROR	06502	−6502	It is raised when an arithmetic, conversion, truncation, or size-constraint error occurs.
ZERO_DIVIDE	01476	1476	It is raised when an attempt is made to divide a number by zero.

Now, we will understand how to define user-defined exceptions followed by how to raise them.

7.14.3 User-Defined Exceptions

The user-defined exception can be declared using this simple syntax in DECLARE block.

Syntax for user-defined exceptions

1. DECLARE

2. my-exception EXCEPTION;

7.14.4 Raising Exceptions

If a programmer needs to raise any exception manually, the RAISE keyword is used to do so. Below is the syntax for raising an exception followed by an example.

Syntax for raising an exception:

1. DECLARE

2. my-exception EXCEPTION;

3. BEGIN

4. IF condition **THEN**

5. RAISE my-exception;

6. **END** IF;

7. EXCEPTION

8. **WHEN** my-exception **THEN**

9. statement;

10. **END**;

7.15 PL/SQL TRIGGER

Triggers can be understood as a scheduled procedure that happens to execute based upon any event. They are configured and are then automatically executed by DBMS engine without any human intervention. Triggers serve many purposes such as deriving some column values, enforcing referential integrity, event logging, auditing, replication of tables, imposing security authorizations, and preventing invalid transactions.

Triggers are executed on any of the following events and can be denied on table, view, schema, or database:

- A database operation (SERVERERROR, LOGON, LOGOFF, STARTUP, or SHUTDOWN).

- A database definition (DDL) statement (CREATE, ALTER, or DROP).

- A database manipulation (DML) statement (DELETE, INSERT, or UPDATE).

Syntax for creating trigger:

1. **CREATE** [OR REPLACE] **TRIGGER** trigger_name

2. {BEFORE | **AFTER | INSTEAD OF** }

3. {**INSERT** [OR] | **UPDATE** [OR] | **DELETE**}

4. [**OF** column_name]

5. **ON** table_name

6. [REFERENCING OLD **AS** o NEW **AS** n]

7. [**FOR** EACH ROW]

8. **WHEN** (condition)

9. DECLARE

10. Declaration-statements

11. BEGIN

12. Executable-statements

13. EXCEPTION

14. Exception-handling-statements

15. **END;**

- CREATE [OR REPLACE] TRIGGER trigger_name: It creates or replaces an existing trigger with the trigger_name.

- {BEFORE | AFTER | INSTEAD OF}: This specifies when the trigger would be executed. The INSTEAD OF clause is used for creating trigger on a view.

- I NSERT [OR] | UPDATE [OR] | DELETE}: This specifies the DML operation.

- [OF col_name]: This specifies the column name that would be updated.

- [ON table_name]: This specifies the name of the table associated with the trigger.

- [REFERENCING OLD AS o NEW AS n]: This allows you to refer new and old values for various DML statements, like INSERT, UPDATE, and DELETE.

- [FOR EACH ROW]: This specifies a row-level trigger, i.e., the trigger would be executed for each row being affected. Otherwise, the trigger will execute just once when the SQL statement is executed, which is called a table-level trigger.

- WHEN (condition): This provides a condition for rows for which the trigger would fire. This clause is valid only for row-level triggers.

7.15.1 Trigger Example

Let's take a simple example to demonstrate the trigger. In this example, we are using our same EMPLOYEE table:

ID	NAME	AGE	ADDRESS	SALARY
1	Alice	22	California	20,000
2	Bob	23	NY	22,000
3	Mark	21	Georgia	24,000
4	Steven	29	California	26,000
5	Jack	22	Texas	28,000

Create trigger:

Let's take a program to create a row-level trigger for the CUSTOMERS table that would fire for INSERT or UPDATE or DELETE operations performed on the CUSTOMERS table. This trigger will display the salary difference between the old values and new values:

1. **CREATE** OR REPLACE **TRIGGER** display_salary_changes

2. BEFORE **DELETE** OR **INSERT** OR **UPDATE ON** employee

3. **FOR** EACH ROW

4. **WHEN** (NEW.ID > 0)

5. DECLARE

6. sal_diff number;

7. BEGIN

8. sal_diff := :NEW.salary - :OLD.salary;

9. dbms_output.put_line('Old salary: ' || :OLD.salary);

10. dbms_output.put_line('New salary: ' || :NEW.salary);

11. dbms_output.put_line('Salary difference: ' || sal_diff);

12. **END**;

After the execution of the above code at SQL prompt, it produces the following result.

Trigger created.

Check the salary difference by procedure:

Use the following code to get the old salary, new salary, and salary difference after the trigger created.

1. DECLARE

2. total_rows number(2);

3. BEGIN

4. **UPDATE** employee

5. **SET** salary = salary + 5000;

6. IF sql%notfound **THEN**

7. dbms_output.put_line('no customers updated');

8. ELSIF sql%found **THEN**

9. total_rows := sql%rowcount;

10. dbms_output.put_line(total_rows || ' customers updated ');

11. **END** IF;

12. **END**;

Output:

Old salary: 20,000

New salary: 25,000

Salary difference: 5000

Old salary: 22,000

New salary: 27,000

Salary difference: 5000

Old salary: 24,000

New salary: 29,000

Salary difference: 5000

Old salary: 26,000

New salary: 31,000

Salary difference: 5000

Old salary: 28,000

New salary: 33,000

Salary difference: 5000

Old salary: 30,000

New salary: 35,000

Salary difference: 5000

Six customers updated

Note: As many times you executed this code, the old and new both salary is incremented by 5000, and hence, the salary difference is always 5000.

After the execution of the above code again, you will get the following result.

Old salary: 25,000

New salary: 30,000

Salary difference: 5000

Old salary: 27,000

New salary: 32,000

Salary difference: 5000

Old salary: 29,000

New salary: 34,000

Salary difference: 5000

Old salary: 31,000

New salary: 36,000

Salary difference: 5000

Old salary: 33,000

New salary: 38,000

Salary difference: 5000
Old salary: 35,000
New salary: 40,000
Salary difference: 5000
Six customers updated

Following are the two very important points and should be noted carefully.

- OLD and NEW references are used for record-level triggers; these are not available for table-level triggers.

If you want to query the table in the same trigger, then you should use the AFTER keyword, because triggers can query the table or change it again only after the initial changes are applied and the table is back in a consistent state.

7.16 SUMMARY

The subject areas of PL/SQL that were discussed include overview of PL/SQL, developing PL/SQL blocks, and controlling process flow with conditional statements and loops, cursors, and error handling. In addition, PL/SQL can be used in four different programming constructs. The types are procedures and functions, packages, and triggers. Procedures and functions are similar in that they both contain a series of instructions that PL/SQL will execute. However, the main difference is that a function will always return one and only one value. Procedures can return more than that number as output parameters. Packages are collected libraries of PL/SQL procedures and functions that have an interface to tell others what procedures and functions are available as well as their parameters, and the body contains the actual code executed by those procedures and functions. Triggers are special PL/SQL blocks that execute when a triggering event occurs. Events that fire triggers include any SQL statement.

Using PL/SQL allows the developer to produce a code that integrates seamlessly with access to the Oracle database. Examples of using all SQL statements, including data selection, data change, and transaction processing statements are given in the chapter. There are no special characters or keywords required for "embedding" SQL statements into PL/SQL, because SQL is an extension of PL/SQL. As such, there really is no embedding at all. Every SQL statement executes in a cursor. When a cursor is not named, it is called an implicit cursor. PL/SQL allows the developer to investigate certain return status features in conjunction with the implicit cursors that run.

Conditional process control is made possible in PL/SQL with the use of if-then-else statements. The if statement uses a Boolean logic comparison to evaluate whether to execute the series of statements after the then clause.

Process flow can be controlled in PL/SQL with the use of loops as well. There are several different types of loops, from simple loop-exit statements to loop-exit when statements, while loop statements, and for loop statements. A simple loop-exit statement consists of the loop and end loop keywords enclosing the statements that will be executed repeatedly, with a special if-then statement designed to identify if an exit condition has been reached. The exit condition is identified in the while clause of the statement. Finally, the for loop statement can be used in cases where the developer wants the code executing repeatedly for a specified number of times.

Cursor manipulation is useful for situations where a certain operation must be performed on each row returned from a query. A cursor is simply an address in memory where a SQL statement executes. A cursor can be explicitly named with the use of the cursor cursor_name is statement, followed by the SQL statement that will comprise the cursor.

The exception handler is arguably the finest feature PL/SQL offers. In it, the developer can handle certain types of predefined exceptions without explicitly coding error-handling routines. The developer can also associate user-defined exceptions with standard Oracle errors, thereby eliminating the coding of an error check in the executable section. This step requires defining the exception using the exception_init pragma and coding a routine that handles the error when it occurs in the exception handler. For completely user-defined errors that do not raise Oracle errors, the user can declare an exception and code a programmatic check in the execution section of the PL/SQL block, followed by some routine to execute when the error occurs in the exception handler.

7.17 REVIEW QUESTIONS

1. How would you reference column values BEFORE and AFTER you have inserted and deleted triggers?

2. How does ROWID help in running a query faster?

3. Write a unique difference between a function and a stored procedure.

4. What are some predefined exceptions in PL/SQL?

5. What are the different schema objects that can be created using PL/SQL?

6. What is the difference between syntax error and runtime error?

7. What is a trigger? Name some instances when "triggers" can be used.

8. What is the importance of %TYPE and %ROWTYPE data types in PL/SQL?

9. Differentiate between the cursors declared in procedures and the cursors declared in the package specifications.

10. What are COMMIT, ROLLBACK, and SAVEPOINT statements in PL/SQL?

11. Write a PL/SQL program using WHILE loop for calculating the average of the numbers entered by the user. Stop the entry of numbers whenever the user enters the number 0.

12. Write a PL/SQL procedure for selecting some records from the database using some parameters as filters.

13. Write a PL/SQL code to find whether a given string is palindrome or not.

14. Write PL/SQL program to convert each digit of a given number into its corresponding word format.

CHAPTER 8

Transaction Management in a Database

8.1 INTRODUCTION

A database is worked upon using transactions, which are small sets of actions aimed at accessing and modifying the state of a database. While working with a database and its associated transactions, it is imperative that the transactions are managed in a smooth, seamless, and trustworthy manner. In this chapter, we cover the different concepts governing the management of transactions in a database. The definition and properties of a transaction with respect to a database are discussed first, followed by different concurrency control mechanisms. Deadlock avoidance, detection, and prevention are discussed next, and the chapter is concluded with discussion around security, integrity and authorization.

8.2 DEFINITION OF TRANSACTION

A database is quite often used by multiple users at a given point in time. While working with a database, a user will interact with the database to achieve an outcome. This interaction with a database is a series of logical steps that are executed sequentially. These are called transactions. End users interact with a database using a set of transactions, which is designed

DOI: 10.1201/9780429282843-8

to carry out a task such as depositing money and buying an item from a website.

Using transactions makes it easier for the database to handle a set of tasks. However, in real world, when a database is accessed concurrently by multiple users at a time, it implies that multiple transactions are taking place for multiple users on a single database at a given point in time. This concurrent access of users to the database creates some problems such as incorrect states and false data transmission to users. In order to solve this problem, we take the route of transaction management with a series of predefined measures, which reduce the possibility of error and inconsistent state.

Transactions can also be considered as the means to access, modify, and manipulate a database. This happens using either the read operation or the write operation on the database using transactions. Let us understand the concept of transaction management using the standard example of transferring money from user A to user B. If user A wants to transfer 2000 rupees to user B, then there must be a deduction in A's account with an addition in B's account. The series of steps which must be followed to perform this transaction are listed as follows:

- Read the account balance of A to check if sufficient balance is there or not.

- Execute the given operation, i.e., $A = A - 2000$.

- Write the newly calculated balance to A's account by overwriting the previous balance.

- Read the account balance of B.

- Execute the given operation, i.e., $B = B + 2000$.

- Write the newly calculated balance to B's account by overwriting the previous balance.

All of the above steps constitute a *transaction* on a database. While working with a large number of end users and a database, chances are that the transactions will collide. What if the user A executed the same transaction 3 times when his balance allows only one? What if there is a power failure or an internet discussion while the user is in the middle of a transaction? In our case, if the transaction fails at the middle, then the user A's balance will be deducted with no addition to user B's account balance.

Such problems lead to a very inconsistent state within the database and may lead to data discrepancy.

The problem of inconsistency is solved by using two specific operations, i.e., commit and rollback.

8.2.1 Commit

Commit operation says that if the transaction reaches the end of the defined order, only then write to the database. In our case, if B's balance is updated, only then the transaction will be added to the database. If the transaction does not reach the end of a defined order of steps, then commit operation will not take place.

In order to adhere to commit operation, all the transactions happening at a given point are kept in the volatile memory of the system. Once the transaction reaches the end of execution, only then the entire transaction is updated in the database. This is the commit operation, and it writes to the database permanently. If a transaction needs to be reversed, it has to be executed again reversing the transaction and then committing again to the database.

Commit operation makes sure that no incomplete transaction is reflected in the database. It is very useful for maintaining the consistency of a database and putting a check on transactions, which might disturb the state of a database.

8.2.2 Rollback

If commit provides the power to update the transaction in a database, then rollback provides the power to revoke a transaction completely. Rollback operation is used to undo the changes that incomplete transactions might have made.

For instance, if the balance is not added to B's account, then those transactions won't be added to the database as commit won't allow them to. However, A's balance will still be deducted in this transaction. This again creates a state of inconsistency at user's end. Rollback operation solves this issue by providing the ability of *rolling back* the transactions, i.e., the executed changes will be undone. In our case, rollback operation will add 2000 to the account of A which was deducted. The incomplete transactions are all rolled back to undo such changes.

In a way, commit and rollback are complementary operations where one is used to permanently write to a database while the other is used to revoke the transactions.

8.3 PROPERTIES OF TRANSACTION

Transactions serve as a meaningful way to operate on a database, as we just learned. There are certain properties that every transaction must follow. These properties are chosen by careful deliberation and are meant to maintain the state of a database to avoid any discrepancy. Adhering to these properties while designing a transaction will allow you to preserve the state of a database without having hung, incomplete, or inconsistent transactions. These properties are commonly called ACID properties, i.e., Atomicity, Consistency, Isolation, and Durability. They are explained as follows:

8.3.1 Atomicity

- Atomicity refers to the property of completion, i.e., whether a transaction completes or it is not executed at all. Commit and rollback operations are designed to maintain the atomicity of the database. If a transaction reaches the end, it is committed to the database, whereas if a transaction is not completed, it is rolled back. Atomicity refers to the atomic nature of a transaction. Even though a transaction is a series of sequential actions, it is considered as atomic and one with all of those actions combined together.

8.3.2 Consistency

- Consistency refers to the correctness of a database. It governs the fact that a given database must be in a consistent state before as well as after the transaction. If a given amount is deducted from a user account, then it must be added somewhere to maintain the overall state of the system. Consistency property maintains that the database stays consistent for such transactions.

8.3.3 Isolation

- Isolation refers to the property of allowing a transaction to execute independently with no interference from other transactions. For instance, if four users are trying to add money to a user's account, then these transactions must not interfere with one another. One must execute after the other, and these must not be aware of the parallel transactions. Isolation guarantees that multiple transactions occurring concurrently will lead to the same effect of the transactions executed sequentially on the database.

8.3.4 Durability

- Durability property ensures that every completed transaction is maintained in a database, and the information is not lost even when the system crashes or an untimely event occurs. Transactions that were wrongly executed in the database are not rolled back. Rather, durability assures that if a transaction is completed, then it must be present in the database, and if the transaction was wrongly executed, then another transaction must be executed to undo the changes. The overall effects of every completed transaction are thus maintained in the database and make it a durable one to work with.

8.4 STATES OF TRANSACTION

Transactions are the bread and butter for database management. Any transaction on a database can be in any one of the following given states at a point in time [1]. These states define the behavior of a transaction as in how a given transaction will proceed further. The transition of a transaction between multiple states is represented in Figure 8.1. Start and end represent the beginning and end of a transaction as shown in the figure. All of the states and their interactions when combined represent the life cycle of a transaction in a database.

8.4.1 Active State

- This is the first state in the lifecycle of the transaction. When a transaction starts execution, it enters the active state. It stays here as long as the sequential steps within the transaction are executed. While executing, the transaction will make certain changes to the state of a database. These changes are stored in buffered memory temporarily.

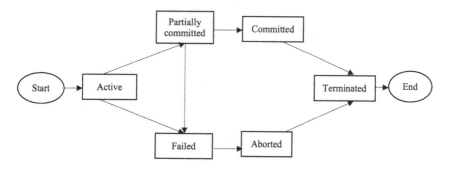

FIGURE 8.1 States of a transaction.

8.4.2 Partially Committed State

- Once the transaction completes execution in the active state, it enters the partially committed state. This state is so named because the transaction is not yet complete and hence partially executed. The transaction is not completed until and unless the changes are reflected in the database. A transaction with changes written in buffer memory is called a partially committed transaction as the changes are not reflected in the database.

8.4.3 Committed State

- Once the transaction executes properly and is ready to be committed to a database, it enters the committed state. This state deals with writing and reflecting the changes of a transaction within the database. Once a transaction reaches this state, it cannot be rolled back. If one has to revoke the changes, a new transaction with given reverted changes must be executed.

8.4.4 Failed State

- When a given transaction is executing in an active state or is present in the partially committed state, if any abrupt event happens, then the transaction moves to the failed state, and the changes are not reflected in the database.

8.4.5 Aborted State

- Once the transaction enters a failed state, the changes made by the transaction must be undone. This is done by rolling back the transaction and then entering the aborted state.

8.4.6 Terminated State

- This is the last state in the lifecycle of a transaction. Whether a transaction completes execution or doesn't, it will always reach the terminated state. This represents the closure of a given transaction.

Every new transaction goes through these states while executing. Every transaction will begin at *start* and arrive at *end*, not matter which route is taken. The goal for transaction execution is the same; they must stick to

ACID properties and preserve the integrity as well as consistency of the database.

8.5 SCHEDULE

We know that transactions are a set of instructions, and these instructions perform operations on a database. When multiple transactions are running concurrently, then there needs to be a sequence in which the operations are performed because at a time, only one operation can be performed on the database. This sequence of operations is known as schedule.

The following sequence of operations is a schedule. Here, we have two transactions T1 and T2 running concurrently.

This schedule determines the exact order of operations that are going to be performed on a database. In this example, all the instructions of transaction T1 are executed before the instructions of transaction T2; however, this is not always necessary, and we can have various types of schedules, which we will discuss in detail.

T1	T2
R(X)	
W(X)	
R(Y)	
	R(Y)
	R(X)
	W(Y)

8.5.1 Types of Schedules

8.5.1.1 Serial Schedule

In **serial schedule**, a transaction is executed completely before starting the execution of another transaction. In other words, we can say that in a serial schedule, a transaction does not start execution until the currently running transaction finishes execution. This type of execution of transaction is also known as **noninterleaved** execution. The example we have seen above is the serial schedule.

Example

Here, R refers to the read operation, and W refers to the write operation. In this example, the transaction T2 does not start execution until the completion of T1.

T1	T2
R(X)	
W(X)	
R(Y)	
	R(Y)
	R(X)
	W(Y)

8.5.1.2 Concurrent Schedule

In concurrent schedule, more than one transactions are running simultaneously.

Example

Consider two transactions T1 and T2. The write operation of transaction T1 precedes the read operation of transaction T2. In the following schedule, both the transactions are running simultaneously, so it is called current schedule.

T1	T2
R(X)	
	R(Y)
W(X)	
	R(Y)
	R(X)
	W(Y)

8.5.1.3 Cascadeless Schedule

In cascadeless schedule, if a transaction is going to perform read operation on a value, it has to wait until the transaction that is performing write on that value commits.

Example

For example, let's say we have transactions T1, T2, and T3. T2 is going to read the value X after the W(X) of T1; then, T2 has to wait for the commit operation of transaction T1 before it reads X.

T1	T2	T3
R(X)		
W(X)		
Commit		
	R(X)	
	W(X)	
	Commit	
		R(X)
		W(X)
		Commit

8.5.1.4 Recoverable Schedule

In recoverable schedule, if a transaction is reading a value which has been updated by some other transaction, then this transaction can commit only after the commit of other transaction which is the updating value.

Recoverable Schedule Example

Here, T2 is performing read operation on X after T1 has made changes in X using W(X), so T2 can only commit after the commit operation of T1.

T1	T2
R(X)	
W(X)	
	R(X)
	W(X)
	R(X)
Commit	
	Commit

8.6 SERIALIZABILITY

A schedule S of n transactions is serializable if it is equivalent to some serial schedule of the same n transaction.

A nonserial schedule S is equivalent to saying that it is correct, because it is equivalent to a serial schedule.

There are two types of serializable schedule

- Conflict-serializable schedule

- View-serializable schedule

8.6.1 Conflict-Serializable Schedule

When the schedule (S) is conflict equivalent to some serial schedule (S'), then that schedule is called conflict-serializable schedule. In such a case, we can reorder the nonconflicting operations in S until we form the equivalent serial schedule **S'**.

T1	T2
R(X)	
W(X)	
R(Y)	
W(Y)	
	R(X)
	W(X)
	R(Y)
	W(Y)

T1	T2
R(X)	
W(X)	
	R(Y)
	W(Y)
R(X)	
W(X)	
	R(Y)
	W(Y)

Serial Schedule Equivalent Concurrent Schedule

The schedules S1 and **S2** are said to be conflict equivalent, if the following conditions are satisfied

- Both schedules S1 and S2 involve the same set of transactions (including ordering of operations within each transaction).

- The order of each pair of conflicting actions in S1 and S2 are the same.

- Then swap the nonconflicting instructions.

If both the transactions are dealing with different data items, then there will be no conflict so we can swap them to achieve the serial schedule, for example, if T1 is reading the value of A data item and T2 is reading the value of B data item, since both are the same, we can swap them.

If both the transactions are dealing with the same data item, then we have to check the conflict as per the following.

a. If Ti issues R(X) and Tj issues R(X), then no conflict as both the transactions are reading the value of X.

b. If Ti issues R(X) and Tj issues W(X), then conflict

c. If Ti issues W(X) and Tj issues R(X), then conflict

d. If Ti issues W(X) and Tj issues W(X), then conflict

In the above concurrent schedule, we can see that all are nonconflicting instructions, so we will swap them, and as a result, we get the equivalent serial schedule.

8.6.2 Precedence Graph Method of Serializability

There is a simple algorithm that can be used to test a schedule for conflict serializability. This algorithm constructs a precedence graph (or serialization graph), which is a directed graph.
   A precedence graph for a schedule S contains the following:

a. A node for each transaction

b. An edge from T_i to Tj if an action of Ti precedes and conflicts with one of Tj's operations, for example, if Ti reads the value of X and then Tj is doing W(x), then there in conflict and an edge from Ti to Tj

T1	T2	T3
R(X)		
	W(X)	
W(X)		
		W(X)

A schedule S is conflict serializable if and only if its precedence graph is acyclic (Figure 8.2).

8.6.3 View-Serializable Schedule

A schedule is view-serializable if it is view-equivalent to some serial schedule.
   Conflict serializable => View serializable, but not vice versa.

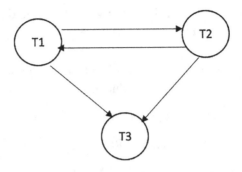

FIGURE 8.2   Precedence graph.

Two schedules S_1 and S2 are view-equivalent:

i. If T_i reads the initial value of the database object **A** in schedule S_1, then T_i also reads the initial value of the database object **A** in schedule S_2.

ii. If T_j reads the value of A written by T_i in schedule S_1, then Tj also reads the value of A written by T_i in schedule S_2.

iii. If T_j writes the final value of A in schedule S_1, then **T_j** also writes the final value of A in S_2.

Schedule S1

T1	T2	T3
R(A)		
	W(A)	
W(A)		
		W(A)

Schedule S2

T1	T2	T3
R(A)		
	W(A)	
		W(A)

In the above example, both schedules S1 and S2 are view-serializable schedules. But S1 schedule is not conflict-serializable schedule, and S2 is not conflict-serializable schedule, because a cycle is not formed.

8.7 RECOVERABLE SCHEDULE

Once a transaction **T** is committed, it should never be necessary to roll back T. The schedules under this criteria are called recoverable schedules, and those that are not are called nonrecoverable schedules.

A schedule **S** is recoverable if no transaction T in S commits until all transactions T' that have written an item that **T** reads have committed.

8.8 CONCURRENCY CONTROL

For a multiuser system, there are high chances that multiple users will operate on a database concurrently. Reading a database concurrently by multiple users does not pose any problem or a threat to a database's consistency [2]. However, things do get tricky when write operations are involved by multiple users at a time. This leads to an inconsistent database state. Let us understand these problems using the following issues that arise due to the same.

8.8.1 Lost Update Problem

- This problem arises when two different read/write operations are executed on the database in a nonconsistent manner leading to an incorrect value updation. Consider the following order of transactions for user A where two transactions are conducted concurrently. T_a reads the balance for user A and subtracts 4000 rupees. This transaction is stored in buffered memory. Meanwhile, T_b reads the balance at t_3, which shows balance as (A-4000) and further adds 2000 rupees to the balance. At t_6, T_a writes the transaction, and at t_7, T_b writes the transaction, thus overwriting the changes done by T_a at t_6. This is the problem created by lost update.

Time	T_a	T_b
t_1	Read(userA)	--
t_2	A = A − 4000;	--
t_3	--	Read(userA)
t_4	--	A = A − 2000;
t_5	--	--
t_6	Write(userA)	--
t_7	--	Write(userA)

8.8.2 Dirty Read Problem

- This problem arises when a rolled-back transaction is read by another transaction before the rollback is complete. Consider the following order of transactions where T_a is reading and then writing a transaction. This updated transaction is read by T_b at t_4. At t_5, the transaction T_a is rolled back, and the value is updated again, but the transaction T_b is operated without accounting for this change. This problem is called dirty read problem as the inconsistency arose because of a read operation, which was later changed.

Time	T_a	T_b
t_1	Read(userA)	--
t_2	A=A+7000	--
t_3	Write(userA)	--
t_4	--	Read(userA)
t_5	Transaction Rollback	--

8.8.3 Inconsistent Retrieval or Unrepeatable Read Problem

This problem arises when a transaction(s) reads different values from the database. Consider the following order of actions for T_a and T_b. The transaction T_a reads the value at t_1 and at t_5. Meanwhile, transaction T_b reads the value and manipulated it post which it is read by T_a again. The problem magnifies while handling multiple users for a given database with high read and write transactions.

Time	T_a	T_b
t_1	Read(userA)	--
t_2	--	Read(userA)
t_3	--	A=A+2500
t_4	--	Write(userA)
t_5	Read(userA)	--

To resolve these problems and maintain the state of a database, concurrency control mechanisms are used. There are practically no issues while dealing with read transactions only. However, while working with write operations, the need for concurrency control arises, which serves as the dedicated mechanism to handle the problems outlined above. This is discussed in detail in the next section.

8.9 CONCURRENCY CONTROL MECHANISM

The concurrency control mechanism provides a means to maintain the atomicity, integrity, consistency, isolation, and durability for a database to allow smooth transaction for end users. There are many ways to achieve concurrency control, some of which are explained as follows:

8.9.1 Lock-Based Protocol

Lock-based protocols propose the use of a lock, which must be acquired by a transaction before it can read or write data for a transaction. This makes sure that the transaction operates in an independent manner without any scope of interference from other transactions. The locks can be of two types, i.e., binary and exclusive/shared locks. Binary locks allow only two states: either it is locked, or it is unlocked. Exclusive/shared locks allow the use of different types of locks for read and write transactions. For read transactions, shared locks can be used as they won't interfere with one another, whereas for write transactions, exclusive lock must be acquired, which prevents sharing. There are numerous ways of using lock-based protocols such as simplistic lock protocol, preclaim lock protocol, and two-phase lock protocol. Simplistic lock protocol provides locks for every write transaction, and the lock is released once the transaction is committed. For preclaim lock protocol, the transaction has to request locks on certain resources. The transaction will wait until it receives lock on all the resources that it needs to execute. For two-phase lock protocol, a transaction has to divide its execution into three steps. First, the resources are listed, and the lock is acquired. Second, the transaction is executed using the locked resources. Third, the resources are released, and write operations are restricted for this transaction.

8.9.1.1 Lock-Based Protocols

A lock is a variable associated with a data item that describes the status of the data item with respect to possible operation that can be applied to it. It synchronizes the access by concurrent transactions to the database items. It is required in this protocol that all the data items must be accessed in a mutually exclusive manner. Let me introduce you to two common locks that are used and some terminologies followed in this protocol.

1. **Shared Lock (S):** It is also known as read-only lock. As the name suggests, it can be shared between transactions because while holding this lock, the transaction does not have the permission to update data on the data item. S-lock is requested using lock-S instruction.

206 Database Management System

2. **Exclusive Lock (X):** Data item can be both read as well as written. This is exclusive and cannot be held simultaneously on the same data item. X lock is requested using lock-X instruction.

Lock-Compatibility Matrix

	S	X
Shared (S)	YES	NO
Exclusive (X)	NO	NO

- A transaction may be granted a lock on an item if the requested lock is compatible with locks already held on the item by other transactions.

- Any number of transactions can hold shared locks on an item, but if any transaction holds an exclusive (X) on the item, no other transaction may hold any lock on the item.

- If a lock cannot be granted, the requesting transaction is made to wait till all incompatible locks held by other transactions have been released. Then the lock is granted.

8.9.1.2 Deadlock Problem with Lock-Based Protocol
Consider the partial schedule:

T1	T2
Lock-X(B)	
read(B)	
Write(B)	
	Lock-S(A)
	Read (A)
	Lock-S(B)
Lock-X(A)	

Deadlock: In the above schedule, we can see two transactions T1 and T2. Initially, T1 is holding exclusive lock on B and starts executing data item B; meanwhile, T2 is requesting shared lock on A and gets the same and starts executing. Now, T2 requesting shared lock on B, but permission not granted because lock is with T1. Similarly, T1 is requesting exclusive lock on A, but permission is not granted due to lock currently held by T2. In the above scenario, both the transactions have to wait for each other, and such a situation is called deadlock.

Starvation: It is also possible if concurrency control manager is badly designed. For example: A transaction may be waiting for an X lock on an item, while a sequence of other transaction requests and are granted an S-lock on the same item. This may be avoided if the concurrency control manager is properly designed.

8.9.1.3 Two-Phase Locking Protocol

Two-phase locking protocol, also known as 2PL protocol, is a method of concurrency control in a DBMS that ensures serializability by applying a lock to the transaction data, which blocks other transactions to access the same data simultaneously. Two-phase locking protocol helps to eliminate the concurrency problem in a DBMS.

This locking protocol divides the execution phase of a transaction into three different parts.

- In the first phase, when the transaction begins to execute, it requires permission for the locks it needs.

- The second part is where the transaction obtains all the locks. When a transaction releases its first lock, the third phase starts.

- In this third phase, the transaction cannot demand any new lock. Instead, it only releases the acquired locks (Figure 8.3).

The two-phase locking protocol allows each transaction to make a lock or unlock request in two steps:

- **Growing Phase**: In this phase, transaction may obtain locks but may not release any locks.

- **Shrinking Phase**: In this phase, a transaction may release locks but not obtain any new lock.

It is true that the 2PL protocol offers serializability. However, it does not ensure that deadlocks do not happen.

In the diagram given above, you can see that local and global deadlock detectors are searching for deadlocks and solve them with resuming transactions to their initial states.

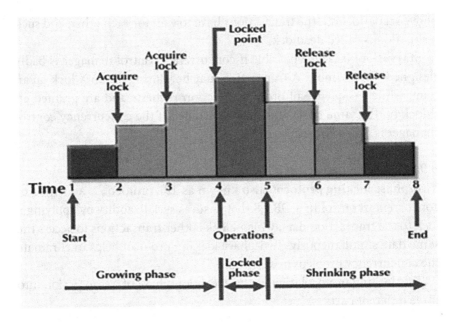

FIGURE 8.3   Two-phase locking.

8.9.2 Timestamp-Based Protocol

Timestamp-based protocols provide a fixed time window for a transaction to execute. The protocol can use a standard time for operating and allotting time to transactions. As soon as a transaction is initiated, it is allotted a timestamp using which it is executed. Transactions that are older get priority over the newly initiated transactions. Every transaction gets the details about the latest read-write operation that was performed on the data item, which the transaction is working on. A more refined version of the timestamp-based protocol is the timestamp ordering protocol, which is used to ensure serializability among transactions. It provides ordering of transactions according to the time stamp value to avoid any overlapping or interference of transactions.

8.9.2.1 Timestamp Ordering Protocol

The main idea of this protocol is to order the transactions based on their timestamps. A schedule in which the transactions participate is then serializable, and the only *equivalent serial schedule permitted* has the transactions in the order of their timestamp values. Stating simply, the schedule is equivalent to the particular *serial order* corresponding to the *order of the transaction timestamps*. An algorithm must ensure that for each item accessed by *conflicting operations* in the schedule, the order in which the item is accessed does not violate the ordering. To ensure this, use two timestamp values relating to each database item **X**.

- **W_TS(X)** is the largest timestamp of any transaction that executed **write(X)** successfully.

- **R_TS(X)** is the largest timestamp of any transaction that executed **read(X)** successfully.

8.9.2.2 Basic Timestamp Ordering

Every transaction is issued a timestamp based on when it enters the system. Suppose, if an old transaction T_i has timestamp $TS(T_i)$, a new transaction T_j is assigned timestamp $TS(T_j)$ such that $\textbf{TS(T}_i\textbf{)} < \textbf{TS(T}_j\textbf{)}$. The protocol manages concurrent execution such that the timestamps determine the serializability order. The timestamp ordering protocol ensures that any conflicting read and write operation is executed in timestamp order. Whenever some transaction T tries to issue a R_item(X) or a W_item(X), the basic TO algorithm compares the timestamp of T with **R_TS(X) & W_TS(X)** to ensure that the timestamp order is not violated. This describes the basic TO protocol in the following two cases.

1. Whenever a transaction T issues a **W_item(X)** operation, check the following conditions:

   - If *R_TS(X) > TS(T)* or if *W_TS(X) > TS(T)*, then abort and roll back T, and reject the operation.

   - Else, execute W_item(X) operation of T and set W_TS(X) to TS(T).

2. Whenever a transaction T issues a **R_item(X)** operation, check the following conditions:

   - If *W_TS(X) > TS(T)*, then abort and reject T, and reject the operation.

   - Else, if W_TS(X) <= TS(T), then execute the R_item(X) operation of T and set R_TS(X) to the larger of TS(T) and current R_TS(X).

Whenever the basic TO algorithm detects two conflicting operations that occur in an incorrect order, it rejects the latter of the two operations by

FIGURE 8.4   Precedence graph for TS ordering.

aborting the transaction that issued it. Schedules produced by basic TO are guaranteed to be *conflict serializable*.

One drawback of the basic TO protocol is that **cascading rollback** is still possible. Suppose we have a transaction T_1, and T_2 has used a value written by T_1. If T_1 is aborted and resubmitted to the system, then T must also be aborted and rolled back. So, the problem of cascading aborts still prevails (Figure 8.4).

Let's gist the advantages and disadvantages of the basic TO protocol:

- Timestamp ordering protocol ensures serializability since the precedence graph will be of the form:

- Timestamp protocol ensures freedom from deadlock as no transaction ever waits.

- But the schedule may *not be cascade free* and may not even be recoverable.

8.9.3 Multiple Granularity-Based Protocols

Multiple granularity-based protocols allow the break up or division of a database into different small blocks or granules. These blocks comprise the database when combined but provide a per-block access for transactions to work on. It involves breaking a database into granules and implementing locking for transaction execution. Using this scheme, concurrency and overhead of transaction is reduced. The division makes the transaction management easier. For locking, intention shared, intention exclusive, shared intention exclusive, or compatibility matrix with intention lock can be used. Intention shared locks allow explicit locking for smaller blocks on a shared basis. Intention exclusive locks allow explicit locking on an exclusive and shared bases. Shared and intention exclusive lock allows shared lock on a resource or a block along with an exclusive lock on a resource or a block.

For example, consider the tree, which consists of four levels of nodes. The highest level represents the entire database. Below it is nodes of type

area; the database consists of exactly these areas. The area has children nodes, which are called files. Every area has those files that are its child nodes. No file can span more than one area.

Finally, each file has child nodes called records. As before, the file consists of exactly those records that are its child nodes, and no record can be present in more than one file. Hence, the levels starting from the top level are as follows (Figure 8.5):

- database

- area

- file

- record

Consider the above diagram for the example given; each node in the tree can be locked individually. As in the two-phase locking protocol, it shall use shared and exclusive lock modes. When a transaction locks a node, in either shared or exclusive mode, the transaction also implicitly locks all the descendants of that node in the same lock mode. For example, if transaction T_i gets an explicit lock on file F_c in exclusive mode, then it has an implicit lock in exclusive mode on all the records belonging to that file. It does not need to lock the individual records of F_c explicitly. This is the main difference between tree-based locking and hierarchical locking for multiple granularities.

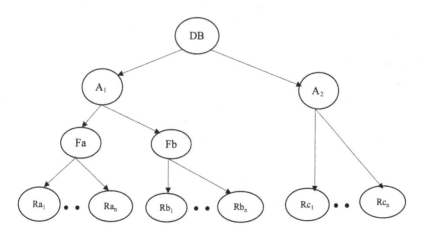

FIGURE 8.5   Multigranularity tree hierarchy.

Now, with locks on files and records made simple, how does the system determine if the root node can be locked? One possibility is for it to search the entire tree but the solution nullifies the whole purpose of the multiple-granularity locking scheme. A more efficient way to gain this knowledge is to introduce a new lock mode, called *intention lock mode.*

8.9.4 Intention Lock Mode

In addition to **S** and **X** lock modes, there are three additional lock modes with multiple granularities:

- **Intention-Shared (IS)**: explicit locking at a lower level of the tree but only with shared locks.

- **Intention-Exclusive (IX)**: explicit locking at a lower level with exclusive or shared locks.

- **Shared and Intention-Exclusive (SIX)**: the subtree rooted by that node is locked explicitly in shared mode, and explicit locking is being done at a lower level with exclusive mode locks (Figure 8.6).

The compatibility matrix for these lock modes is described below:

	IS	IX	S	SIX	X
IS	YES	YES	YES	YES	NO
IX	YES	YES	NO	NO	NO
S	YES	NO	YES	NO	NO
SIX	YES	NO	NO	NO	NO
X	NO	NONO	NO	NO	NO

IS: Intention Shared, X: Exclusive, IX: Intention Exclusive, SIX: Shared& Intention Exclusive, S: Shared

The multiple-granularity locking protocol uses the intention lock modes to ensure serializability. It requires that a transaction T_i that attempts to lock a node must follow these protocols:

1. Transaction T_i must follow the lock-compatibility matrix.

2. Transaction T_i must lock the root of the tree first, and it can lock it in any mode.

	IS	IX	S	SIX	X
IS	YES	YES	YES	YES	NO
IX	YES	YES	NO	NO	NO
S	YES	NO	YES	NO	NO
SIX	YES	NO	NO	NO	NO
X	NO	NONO	NO	NO	NO

FIGURE 8.6   Multigranularity tree hierarchy.

3. Transaction T_i can lock a node in S or IS mode only if T_i currently has the parent of the node locked in either IX or IS mode.

4. Transaction T_i can lock a node in X, SIX, or IX mode only if T_i currently has the parent of the node locked in either IX or SIX modes.

5. Transaction T_i can lock a node only if T_i has not previously unlocked any node (i.e., T_i is two-phase).

6. Transaction T_i can unlock a node only if T_i currently has none of the children of the node locked.

Observe that the multiple-granularity protocol requires that locks be acquired in top-down (root-to-leaf) order, whereas locks must be released in bottom-up (leaf to-root) order.

As an illustration of the protocol, consider the tree given above and the transactions:

• Say transaction T_1 reads record R_{a2} in file F_a. Then, T_2 needs to lock the database, area A_1, and F_a in IS mode (and in that order) and finally to lock R_{a2} in S mode.

• Say transaction T_2 modifies record R_{a9} in file F_a. Then, T_2 needs to lock the database, area A_1, and file F_a (and in that order) in IX mode and at last to lock R_{a9} in X mode.

- Say transaction T_3 reads all the records in file F_a. Then, T_3 needs to lock the database and area A_1 (and in that order) in IS mode and at last to lock F_a in S mode.

- Say transaction T_4 reads the entire database. It can do so after locking the database in S mode.

8.9.5 Multiversion Schemes

As the abovementioned approaches use locks to work with, multiversion schemes offer a new approach. It provides the end user with a consistent snapshot of the database to work with. No transaction has to wait in this case for acquiring locks before they can execute. Different users can thereby concurrently operate with the version provided to them. After a given time, the database is cumulatively set and made consistent again.

There can be multiple different ways to exercise control of concurrency preserving mechanisms for a database. We just explained a few major categories of them. A good concurrency control mechanism must be resilient and persevere through threats such as system failure and communication loss. It must allow a smooth parallel or concurrent execution of multiple transactions with a minimum possible overhead.

8.9.5.1 Multiversion Concurrency Control Techniques

Multiversion concurrency control techniques keep the old values of a data item when the item is updated. Several versions (values) of an item are maintained. When a transaction requires access to an item, an appropriate version is chosen to maintain the serializability of the concurrently executing schedule, if possible. The idea is that some read operations that would be rejected in other techniques can still be accepted by reading an older version of the item to maintain serializability.

An obvious drawback of multiversion techniques is that more storage is needed to maintain multiple versions of the database items. However, older versions may have to be maintained, for example, for recovery purpose. In addition, some database applications require older versions to be kept to maintain a history of the evolution of data item values. The extreme case is a temporal database, which keeps track of all changes and the items at which they occurred. In such cases, there is no additional penalty for multiversion techniques, since older versions are already maintained.

8.9.5.2 Multiversion Techniques Based on Timestamp Ordering
In his technique, several versions X1, X2, ...Xk of each data item X are kept by the system. For each version, the value of version Xi and the following two timestamps are kept:

1. read_TS(Xi): The read timestamp of Xi; this is the largest of all the timestamps of transactions that have successfully read version Xi.

2. write_TS(Xi): The write timestamp of Xi; this is the timestamp of the transaction that wrote the value of version Xi.

Whenever a transaction T is allowed to execute a write_item(X) operation, a new version of item X, Xk+1, is created, with both the write_TS(Xk+1) and the read_TS(Xk+1) set to TS(T). Correspondingly, when a transaction T is allowed to read the value of version Xi, the value of read_TS(Xi) is set to the largest of read_TS(Xi) and TS(T).

To ensure serializability, we use the following two rules to control the reading and writing of data items:

1. If transaction T issues a write_item(X) operation, and version i of X has the highest write_TS(Xi) of all versions of X which is also less than or equal to TS(T), and TS(T) < read_TS(Xi), then abort and rollback transaction T; otherwise, create a new version Xj of X with read_TS(Xj) = write_TS(Xj) = TS(T).

2. If transaction T issues a read_item(X) operation, and version i of X has the highest write_TS(Xi) of all versions of X which is also less than or equal to TS(T), then return the value of Xi to transaction T, and set the value of read_TS(Xj) to the largest of TS(T) and the current read_TS(Xj).

8.10 DATABASE BACKUP AND RECOVERY

While handling huge databases, it is possible that the data gets lost or compromised due to various hardware- or software-based reasons such as operating system failure, device failure, and application errors. Data backup refers to the copy of data, which can be used when such catastrophic events may happen [3]. Maintaining backups is useful for dealing with such unprecedented events. The process of recovering the loss of data using backups is referred to as database recovery. A database can be recovered partially or fully using the backups, depending upon the need of the database administrator.

A backup can be taken periodically and is generally achieved using physical and logical backups. Physical backup refers to the physical copy of the entire database including data files, control files, and log files. Logical backup on the other hand refers to the logical views and information extracted from the physical database such as tables, functions, views, procedures, and transient transactions conducted on the database generate backups by using logs. A log is a file that records or saves a sequence of steps. Log files are one of the most used backup mechanisms for database backup as well as recovery. Following are the different ways to use log files under different circumstances.

a. **Deferred Database Modification**: It is used for cases where data is lost due to power failure, operating system failure, or system crash. Primarily, it is used for saving transactions that are not immediately reflected in the database. Whenever a transaction starts executing, it is stored within the buffer memory. The changes made by the transaction are not reflected in the database immediately, and they are stored in log files. When an unprecedented event happens, these log files can be used to retrieve the transactions that were complete but not committed in the database. This is called deferred database modification using log files for recovering lost data. The disadvantage to this approach is the time taken to reconstruct the entire database along with the executed transactions.

b. **Immediate Database Modification**: This type of recovery mechanism is used for maintaining the transaction logs for the database. It is used to recover the transactions that are lost due to power failure, OS failure, or application failure. The changes made by a transaction are immediately reflected in the database and are also maintained in the log files. The log files store both the old as well as the new transactions. Log files are used to maintain the state of the database. In case of completed and committed transactions, if a database fails, then it can be recovered by using the log files. If in case the transactions are rolled back, then also the old values can be retrieved using the log files. The disadvantage of using this mechanism is the overhead of writing and rewriting to log files.

c. **Checkpointing**: A checkpoint is used as a means to break up the transaction log for a database. The point of synchronization between the transaction log and the database is called checkpoint [4]. In case of any failure, these checkpoints can be used to retrieve the lost state of a database. Checkpoints are deployed at certain intervals, and at those intervals, the modified transactions are dumped as log files onto the physical disk of the system. These log files segregated using particular check points can then be used to reset the state of a database. It works as a dedicated process that runs at particular intervals. It constantly records the new transactions and flushes out the old ones, thereby leading to low overhead and optimized execution.

8.10.1 Log-Based Recovery

Log is a sequence of records, which maintains the records of actions performed by a transaction. It is important that the logs are written prior to the actual modification and stored on a stable storage media, which is failsafe.

Log-based recovery works as follows:

- The log file is kept on a stable storage media.

- When a transaction enters the system and starts execution, it writes a log about it.
  $<T_n, Start>$

- When the transaction modifies an item X, it write logs as follows:
  $<T_n, X, V_1, V_2>$

It reads T_n has changed the value of X, from V_1 to V_2.

- When the transaction finishes, it logs
  $<T_n, commit>$

The database can be modified using two approaches:

- **Deferred Database Modification**: All logs are written on to the stable storage, and the database is updated when a transaction commits.

- **Immediate Database Modification**: Each log follows an actual database modification. That is, the database is modified immediately after every operation.

8.10.2 Recovery with Concurrent Transactions

When more than one transactions are being executed in parallel, the logs are interleaved. At the time of recovery, it would become hard for the recovery system to backtrack all logs and then start recovering. To ease this situation, most modern DBMSs use the concept of "checkpoints".

8.10.2.1 Checkpoint

Keeping and maintaining logs in real time and in a real environment may fill out all the memory space available in the system. As time passes, the log file may grow too big to be handled at all. Checkpoint is a mechanism where all the previous logs are removed from the system and stored permanently in a storage disk. Checkpoint declares a point before which the DBMS was in consistent state, and all the transactions were committed.

8.10.2.2 Recovery

When a system with concurrent transactions crashes and recovers, it behaves in the following manner (Figure 8.7):

- The recovery system reads the logs backward from the end to the last checkpoint.

- It maintains two lists, an undo list and a redo list.

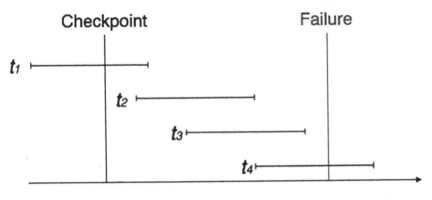

FIGURE 8.7   Checkpointing.

- If the recovery system sees a log with $<T_n,$ Start> and $<T_n,$ Commit> or just $<T_n,$ Commit>, it puts the transaction in the redo list.

- If the recovery system sees a log with $<T_n,$ Start> but no commit or abort log found, it puts the transaction in the undo list.

All the transactions in the undo list are then undone, and their logs are removed. All the transactions in the redo list and their previous logs are removed and then redone before saving their logs.

8.11 SECURITY, INTEGRITY, AND AUTHORIZATION

Security with respect to a database refers to the protection of a database from malicious entities such as malicious, unauthorized, and unauthenticated users. A database's security can be compromised due to many reasons such as unauthorized access and modification, tampering with data, data theft, stealing of passwords, so on and so forth. There are multiple dimensions from where a database can be attacked and manipulated. Normally, a database works on a number of users and that makes it even more important to secure. There can be many threat vectors to a database and considering the criticality of the data stored in a database, it is very important to secure it from every threat possible. Securing the underlying infrastructure including server and networks is one of the starting measures for ensuring security. There can be many database security controls such as access control, authorization and authentication, monitoring, system hardening, and maintaining configuration [5]. Some of these are briefly explained as below:

- **DBMS Configuration Management and Hardening**: Access to a database must be strictly monitored and be done using privileged controls. The configuration of a database must be protected for any unauthorized change to ensure that the entire database is consistent.

- **Authentication**: Authentication is the process of verifying whether a user is the one whose credentials match with their privileges for a given database. It maintains a strict check to ensure that a database is not accessed by malicious users while making sure that genuine users get a smooth access to the database.

- **Backup and Recovery**: Maintaining the security of backup data and the recovery process is equally important as they may serve as doorways for malicious users to attack.

- **Auditing**: Auditing or database monitoring is helpful in detecting, determining, restricting, and easing the overall legal as well as illegal activities within a database. Using proper auditing controls, a database can be made more secure and consistent with an increased detection of threats.

- **Access Control**: It is imperative to monitor and control who is accessing what and how, which all encompass the access control means for a database. Maintaining strict security at user endpoints is critical as these serve as the entry point of manipulation for a database. While malicious users must be blocked, it must be assured that no genuine user suffers any lag due to improper implementation of access control measures.

- **Encryption**: While authentication and authorization, encryption keys are circulated, and protecting them is very important. Managing encryption keys and their generation and circulation serves as a critical component while working on securing a database.

- **Application Security**: Common attacks such as data theft, spoofing, man-in-the-middle attack, denial of service attack, and SQL injection can be handled efficiently while working on application security.

Integrity refers to the accuracy of the data, and maintaining the integrity of a database refers to protection of a database against entities that would modify or tamper with the database leading to compromise in the database integrity. Integrity in a database is maintained using certain rules or procedures. It refers to the structure of the database and its schema, which serves as the backbone for a database. Integrity is mostly implemented using primary key, foreign key constraints, and various checks for relationships between attributes.

8.12 SUMMARY

Concurrency control is the procedure in DBMSs for managing simultaneous operations without conflicting with each another. Lost updates, dirty read, nonrepeatable read, and incorrect summary issue are problems faced due to lack of concurrency control. Lock-based, two-phase, timestamp-based, and validation-based are types of concurrency handling protocols. The lock could be shared (S) or exclusive (X). The two-phase locking protocol also known as a 2PL protocol needs that transaction should acquire a lock after it releases one of its locks. It has two phases: growing and shrinking. The timestamp-based algorithm uses a timestamp to serialize the execution of concurrent transactions. The protocol uses the system time or logical count as a timestamp.

8.13 REVIEW QUESTIONS

1. Explain what is meant by a transaction. Discuss the meaning of transaction states and operations.

2. Discuss the actions taken by the read_item and write_item operations on a database.

3. What is meant by interleaved concurrent execution of database transactions in a multiuser system? Discuss why concurrency control is needed, and give informal examples.

4. Discuss the different types of possible transaction failures with some examples.

5. Transactions cannot be nested inside one another. Why? Support your answer with an example.

6. Compare binary locks with exclusive/shared locks. Why is the latter type of locks preferable?

7. Discuss why the schedule below is a nonserializable schedule. What went wrong with the multiple-mode locking scheme used in the example schedule? (Figure 8.8)

8. Given the graph below, identify the deadlock situations (Figure 8.9).

9. What is the two-phase locking protocol? How does it guarantee serializability?

10. Analyze the relationships among the following terminologies: problems of concurrency access to a database (lost update, uncommitted dependency), serializable schedule, basic 2PL, deadlock, conservative 2PL, and wait-die and wound-wait.

11. How does the granularity of data items affect the performance of concurrency control? What factors affect selection of granularity size for data items?

12. Discuss multiversion two-phase locking for concurrency control.

T1	T2
Read_lock(Y)	
Read_item(Y)	
Unlock(Y)	Read_lock(X)
	Read_item(X)
	Unlock(X)
	Write_lock(Y)
	Read_item(Y)
	Y=X+Y
	Write_item(Y)
	Unlock(Y)
Write_lock(X)	
Read_item(X)	
X=X+Y	
Write_item(X)	
Unlock(X)	

FIGURE 8.8 Schedule example.

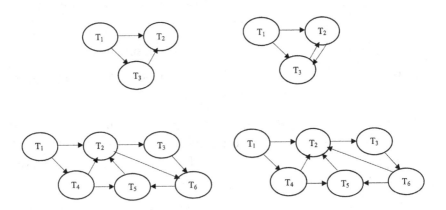

FIGURE 8.9 Deadlock example.

REFERENCES

1. "Transaction States in DBMS - GeeksforGeeks." [Online]. Available: https://www.geeksforgeeks.org/transaction-states-in-dbms/. [Accessed: 06-Jun-2021].
2. "DBMS Concurrency Control - javatpoint." [Online]. Available: https://www.javatpoint.com/dbms-concurrency-control. [Accessed: 06-Jun-2021].
3. "DBMS Deadlock in DBMS - javatpoint." [Online]. Available: https://www.javatpoint.com/deadlock-in-dbms. [Accessed: 06-Jun-2021].
4. "Checkpoints in DBMS - GeeksforGeeks." [Online]. Available: https://www.geeksforgeeks.org/checkpoints-in-dbms/. [Accessed: 06-Jun-2021].
5. "What is Database Security? Definition, Types & Importance | Looker." [Online]. Available: https://looker.com/definitions/database-security. [Accessed: 06-Jun-2021].

Index

Note: *Italic* page numbers refer to figures.

aborted state, transaction 196
accuracy 6
active state, transaction 195
aggregate functions 129–133
airlines 20
Armstrong's axioms 109–110
atomicity 8, 194

bad design, relational database model 32
banking systems 20
binary operators 59
Boyce-Codd normal form (BCNF)
    112–113

candidate keys 52–53, 54
cardinality 31
Cartesian Product 62–63
cascadeless schedule 198–199
casual end users 11
check clause 58
Codd, E. F. 2, 66
Commit command 127
committed state, transaction 196
complex data types, object relational
    database model 36
complexity, object relational database
    model 37
composite keys 53, 54
conceptual level
    data independence 41
    three-level architecture of database
        39, *40*
conceptual simplicity
    network data model 28, 32
    relational database model 32

concurrency control
    dirty read problem 204
    inconsistent retrieval problem 204
    intention lock mode 212–214
    lock-based protocol 205–207, *208*
    lost update problem 203
    multiple granularity-based protocols
        210–212, *211*
    multiversion schemes 214–215
    timestamp-based protocol
        208–210, *210*
concurrent schedule 198
consistency 5, 16
constraints 38
    enhanced entity-relationship model 95
    integrity 55–58
        check clause 58
        default value 58
        domain 57
        entity 55
        null 57–58
        referential 55–56
    SQL 143–144
conversion functions 137–139

data access performance, object-oriented
    data model 35
database
    advantages
        backup and recovery 17
        enforcing integrity constraints 18
        faster data access 17
        multiple user interfaces 17
        persistent storage 18
        preventing unauthorized
            access 16–17

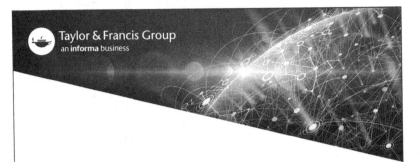

Printed in the United States
by Baker & Taylor Publisher Services